CALEB ROSS

Flask API For mobile App Development

Copyright © 2024 by Caleb Ross

All rights reserved. No part of this publication may be reproduced, stored or transmitted in any form or by any means, electronic, mechanical, photocopying, recording, scanning, or otherwise without written permission from the publisher. It is illegal to copy this book, post it to a website, or distribute it by any other means without permission.

First edition

This book was professionally typeset on Reedsy.
Find out more at reedsy.com

Contents

Part I: Foundations of Flask APIs for Mobile Apps Chapter 1:... 1
Chapter 2: Setting up a Flask Development Environment 13
Chapter 3: Flask API Basics: Routing, Requests, and... 26
Chapter 4: Data Management with Flask-SQLAlchemy 39
Chapter 5: Authentication and Authorization in Flask APIs 49
Part II: Building Production-Ready Flask APIs Chapter 6:... 57
Chapter 7: Versioning and Evolving Flask APIs 70
Chapter 8: Integrating Flask APIs with Mobile Frameworks 78
Chapter 9: Deploying Flask APIs to Cloud Platforms 90
Chapter 10: Extending Flask Capabilities with Extensions 99
Part III: Ensuring Robust Flask API Quality Chapter 11:... 108
Chapter 12: Securing Flask APIs 118
Chapter 13: Monitoring and Troubleshooting Flask APIs 127
Chapter 14: Best Practices and Coding Exercises 136
Chapter 15: Conclusion and Next Steps 146

Part I: Foundations of Flask APIs for Mobile Apps Chapter 1: Introduction to Flask APIs for Mobile Development

In the rapidly evolving world of mobile app development, the need for robust and scalable backend solutions has never been more pressing. Amidst the proliferation of feature-rich mobile applications, developers are increasingly recognizing the importance of a well-designed API infrastructure to power their mobile experiences. It is in this context that Flask, a lightweight and flexible Python web framework, has emerged as a compelling choice for building mobile-focused API backends.

Flask: A Powerful Choice for Mobile API Development

Flask is a minimalist and highly customizable web framework that has gained widespread popularity in the Python development community. Unlike heavyweight frameworks that come with a predefined set of features and conventions, Flask takes a more modular approach, allowing developers to build their applications from the ground up. This flexibility is particularly advantageous when it comes to developing mobile APIs, as it enables developers to tailor the backend solution to the specific needs of their mobile applications.

One of the primary strengths of Flask is its simplicity and ease of use. The framework's streamlined syntax and intuitive API make it approachable for developers of all skill levels, from seasoned professionals to newcomers to the world of web development. This accessibility is crucial in the mobile app development landscape, where teams often need to quickly prototype, iterate, and deploy new features to keep pace with evolving user demands.

Moreover, Flask's minimalist nature translates to a lightweight and efficient runtime, which is a crucial consideration for mobile API backends. Mobile apps often operate in resource-constrained environments, where performance and scalability are paramount. Flask's ability to handle high-volume traffic and respond swiftly to API requests makes it an ideal choice for powering the backend infrastructure of mobile applications.

Common Use Cases and Benefits of Flask-Powered Mobile APIs

The versatility of Flask enables it to address a wide range of use cases in the mobile app development domain. Here are some of the most common scenarios where Flask-powered APIs excel:

1. **Rapid Prototyping and MVP Development**: The simplicity and flexibility of Flask allow developers to quickly build and iterate on mobile backend solutions, enabling the rapid development of minimum viable products (MVPs) and the testing of new ideas.
2. **Microservices-based Architectures**: Flask's modular design lends itself well to the creation of microservices-based API architectures, where individual services can be developed, deployed, and scaled independently to meet the evolving needs of mobile apps.
3. **Integrating with Mobile Platforms**: Flask's compatibility with popular mobile development frameworks, such as React Native, Flutter, and native Android/iOS, makes it an attractive choice for building the backend components that seamlessly integrate with mobile frontends.
4. **Offline-first Experiences**: Flask-powered APIs can be designed to support offline functionality, caching data and synchronizing it with mobile apps when network connectivity is restored, providing a more reliable and enjoyable user experience.
5. **Serverless Deployments**: The lightweight nature of Flask makes it well-suited for serverless deployment models, such as AWS Lambda, where the backend infrastructure is automatically scaled and managed by the cloud provider, reducing the operational overhead for mobile

app developers.

6. **Customizable Authentication and Authorization**: Flask provides a flexible foundation for implementing robust authentication and authorization mechanisms, ensuring that sensitive data and API endpoints are accessible only to authorized mobile app users.
7. **Scalable and High-performance APIs**: Flask's ability to handle high-volume traffic and its integration with powerful database engines, caching solutions, and asynchronous task queues make it a reliable choice for building scalable and high-performance API backends for mobile apps.

By leveraging the strengths of Flask, mobile app developers can build API backends that are not only efficient and scalable but also tailored to the unique requirements of their mobile applications. The framework's simplicity, flexibility, and performance characteristics make it a compelling choice for powering the next generation of innovative mobile experiences.

Chapter 2: Setting up a Flask Development Environment

Establishing a robust and streamlined development environment is a crucial first step in building Flask-powered APIs for mobile applications. This chapter will guide you through the process of setting up a Flask development environment, ensuring that you have the necessary tools and configurations in place to start building and deploying your mobile API solutions.

Installing Flask and Related Dependencies

The foundation of a Flask development environment is, of course, the Flask framework itself. To get started, you'll need to install Flask and its associated dependencies. This can be accomplished using Python's built-in package manager, pip.

Open a terminal or command prompt and run the following command to install the latest version of Flask:

```
Copy
pip install flask
```

In addition to the core Flask framework, you may also need to install other packages and libraries that are commonly used in Flask-powered API development. Some of the most popular and useful dependencies include:

- **Flask-SQLAlchemy**: A Flask extension that provides an Object-Relational Mapping (ORM) layer, simplifying the integration between Flask and various database engines.
- **Flask-JWT-Extended**: A Flask extension that handles token-based authentication, making it easier to implement secure and scalable authentication mechanisms for your mobile APIs.
- **Flask-Migrate**: A Flask extension that manages database schema migrations, allowing you to easily evolve your data models as your mobile app and API requirements change.
- **Flask-RESTful**: A Flask extension that streamlines the process of building RESTful APIs, providing a set of abstractions and conventions to simplify API development.

You can install these dependencies using the same pip install command:

```
Copy
pip install flask-sqlalchemy flask-jwt-extended flask-migrate flask-restful
```

Depending on the specific needs of your mobile API project, you may also need to install additional packages and libraries. The beauty of Flask is its modular nature, allowing you to pick and choose the components that best fit your requirements.

Configuring a Development Workflow

With Flask and its dependencies installed, the next step is to set up a development workflow that will help you write, test, and deploy your mobile API solutions efficiently.

1. **Virtual Environments**: It is highly recommended to use a virtual

environment to manage your project's Python dependencies. This ensures that each project has its own isolated set of installed packages, preventing conflicts and version issues. Tools like virtualenv or pipenv can be used to create and manage virtual environments.
2. **Code Editors and IDEs**: Choosing a suitable code editor or Integrated Development Environment (IDE) can significantly enhance your productivity. Popular options for Flask development include PyCharm, Visual Studio Code, and the Sublime Text editor, all of which provide features like syntax highlighting, code completion, and integrated debugging capabilities.
3. **Version Control**: Implementing a version control system, such as Git, is crucial for managing the codebase of your Flask-powered mobile API. This allows you to track changes, collaborate with team members, and maintain a clear history of your project's development.
4. **Automated Testing**: Establishing a comprehensive testing suite is essential for ensuring the reliability and stability of your mobile API. Flask provides excellent support for writing unit tests, integration tests, and end-to-end tests using frameworks like unittest, pytest, or Postman.
5. **Continuous Integration and Deployment**: To streamline the process of building, testing, and deploying your Flask-powered mobile APIs, consider integrating your project with a Continuous Integration (CI) and Continuous Deployment (CD) platform, such as Travis CI, CircleCI, or GitHub Actions. These tools can automate the build, test, and deployment processes, ensuring that your mobile API is always up-to-date and ready for use.

By setting up a well-structured development workflow, you can ensure that your Flask-powered mobile API project is maintainable, scalable, and ready for production deployment.

Chapter 3: Flask API Basics: Routing, Requests, and Responses

At the core of any Flask-powered mobile API is the ability to define routes, handle HTTP requests, and generate appropriate responses. In this chapter, we will explore the fundamental concepts and techniques for building robust and efficient API endpoints using Flask.

Defining API Endpoints with Flask Routes

The foundation of a Flask-powered API is the creation of routes, which map incoming HTTP requests to the corresponding Python functions that handle the logic and generate the responses. In Flask, you can define routes using the @app.route() decorator, which allows you to specify the URL patterns and the HTTP methods (GET, POST, PUT, DELETE) that the route should accept.

Here's a simple example of how to define a route for a mobile API endpoint:

```python
Copy
from flask import Flask, jsonify

app = Flask(__name__)

@app.route('/users', methods=['GET'])
def get_users():
    users = [
        {'id': 1, 'name': 'John Doe', 'email': 'john.doe@example.com'},
        {'id': 2, 'name': 'Jane Smith', 'email': 'jane.smith@example.com'},
    ]
    return jsonify(users)
```

In this example, the get_users() function is associated with the /users route and the GET HTTP method. When a client sends a GET request to the /users endpoint, Flask will automatically invoke the get_users() function and return the response as a JSON payload.

Handling HTTP Methods in Flask APIs

Flask's routing system allows you to specify which HTTP methods (GET, POST, PUT, DELETE) each endpoint should accept. This flexibility enables you to build RESTful APIs that follow the appropriate HTTP semantics for various CRUD (Create, Read, Update, Delete) operations.

Here's an example of how you can handle different HTTP methods for a user management API:

```python
Copy
from flask import Flask, jsonify, request

app = Flask(__name__)

@app.route('/users', methods=['GET', 'POST'])
def users():
    if request.method == 'GET':
        users = [
            {'id': 1, 'name': 'John Doe', 'email':
            'john.doe@example.com'},
            {'id': 2, 'name': 'Jane Smith', 'email':
            'jane.smith@example.com'},
        ]
        return jsonify(users)
    elif request.method == 'POST':
        new_user = request.get_json()
        # Logic to create a new user and store it in the database
        return jsonify(new_user), 201

@app.route('/users/<int:user_id>', methods=['GET', 'PUT',
'DELETE'])
def user(user_id):
    if request.method == 'GET':
        # Logic to retrieve a specific user by ID
        user = {'id': user_id, 'name': 'John Doe', 'email':
        'john.doe@example.com'}
        return jsonify(user)
    elif request.method == 'PUT':
        # Logic to update an existing user by ID
        updated_user = request.get_json()
        return jsonify(updated_user)
    elif request.method == 'DELETE':
        # Logic to delete a user by ID
        return '', 204
```

In this example, the /users route handles both GET and POST requests, allowing clients to retrieve a list of users or create a new user, respectively. The /users/<int:user_id> route, on the other hand, handles GET, PUT, and DELETE requests, enabling clients to retrieve, update, and delete individual users by their unique identifier.

Parsing and Validating Request Data

When building mobile APIs, it's essential to handle incoming data from client requests effectively. Flask provides several ways to access and validate request data, ensuring that your API endpoints can process valid inputs and handle invalid ones gracefully.

One of the most common approaches is to use the request.get_json() method to retrieve the JSON-formatted data sent in the request body. Here's an example:

```python
Copy
from flask import Flask, jsonify, request
from flask_restful import Api, Resource, reqparse

app = Flask(__name__)
api = Api(app)

class UserResource(Resource):
    def post(self):
        parser = reqparse.RequestParser()
        parser.add_argument('name', type=str, required=True)
        parser.add_argument('email', type=str, required=True)
        args = parser.parse_args()

        # Logic to create a new user in the database using the validated input
        new_user = {'id': 1, 'name': args['name'], 'email': args['email']}
        return jsonify(new_user), 201

api.add_resource(UserResource, '/users')
```

In this example, we're using the flask_restful extension to define a UserResource class that handles the /users endpoint. The post() method uses the reqparse.RequestParser to define the expected parameters (name and email) and their validation rules (required string types). The parser.parse_args() call automatically validates the input data and returns a dictionary of the parsed arguments, which can then be used to create a new user in the database.

By validating the incoming request data, you can ensure that your mobile API endpoints are robust and can handle a variety of client inputs without failing or returning unexpected responses.

Returning Responses from Flask APIs

Once you've processed the incoming request and performed the necessary logic, it's time to return a response to the client. Flask provides several ways to generate and customize the responses, depending on the needs of your mobile API.

The most common approach is to use the jsonify() function, which automatically converts a Python dictionary or list into a JSON-formatted response:

```python
Copy
from flask import Flask, jsonify

app = Flask(__name__)

@app.route('/users/<int:user_id>'
, methods=['GET'])
def get_user(user_id):
    user = {'id': user_id, 'name':
 'John Doe', 'email':
'john.doe@example.com'}
    return jsonify(user)
```

In this example, the get_user() function returns a JSON response containing the user data.

In addition to jsonify(), you can also use the standard Flask.make_response() method to create custom responses, including setting status codes, headers, and even streaming data:

```python
Copy
from flask import Flask, make_response

app = Flask(__name__)

@app.route('/downloads/<filename>', methods=['GET'])
def download_file(filename):
    # Logic to retrieve the file from storage
    file_content = b'This is the content of the file.'

    response = make_response(file_content)
    response.headers.set('Content-Type', 'application/octet-stream')
    response.headers.set('Content-Disposition', 'attachment', filename=filename)
    return response
```

In this example, the download_file() function returns a custom response with a Content-Type header set to application/octet-stream and a Content-Disposition header set to attachment, indicating that the response should be treated as a file download.

By mastering the techniques for defining routes, handling HTTP methods, validating input, and returning responses, you can build robust and efficient mobile API backends using the Flask framework.

Chapter 4: Data Management with Flask-SQLAlchemy

One of the core responsibilities of a mobile API backend is the management and persistence of data. In the Flask ecosystem, the Flask-SQLAlchemy extension provides a powerful and intuitive way to integrate a database into your API, allowing you to define data models, perform CRUD (Create, Read, Update, Delete) operations, and establish relationships between entities.

Integrating a Database with Flask-SQLAlchemy

To get started with Flask-SQLAlchemy, you'll first need to install the extension and configure it within your Flask application:

```python
Copy
from flask import Flask
from flask_sqlalchemy import SQLAlchemy

app = Flask(__name__)
app.config['SQLALCHEMY_DATABASE_URI'] = 'sqlite:///database.db'
db = SQLAlchemy(app)
```

In this example, we're configuring the Flask-SQLAlchemy extension to use a SQLite database stored in a file named database.db. You can also configure Flask-SQLAlchemy to work with other database engines, such as PostgreSQL, MySQL, or Oracle, by modifying the SQLALCHEMY_DATABASE_URI setting accordingly.

Defining Data Models with Flask-SQLAlchemy

Once you've integrated the database, you can start defining your data models using the db.Model class provided by Flask-SQLAlchemy. These models represent the various entities and relationships in your mobile app's data schema.

Here's an example of a simple User model:

```python
Copy
from flask_sqlalchemy import SQLAlchemy

db = SQLAlchemy()

class User(db.Model):
    id = db.Column(db.Integer, primary_key=True)
    name = db.Column(db.String(50), nullable=False)
    email = db.Column(db.String(120), unique=True, nullable=False)
```

```
    password_hash = db.
Column(db.String(100), nullable=False)

    def __repr__(self):
        return f'<User {self.name}>'
```

In this example, the User model has four columns: id, name, email, and password_hash. The db.Column() function is used to define the characteristics of each column, such as the data type, whether it's a primary key, and whether it's required (nullable).

The __repr__() method is a special method that returns a string representation of the model instance, which can be useful for debugging and logging purposes.

Performing CRUD Operations with Flask-SQLAlchemy

With the data models defined, you can now use Flask-SQLAlchemy to perform CRUD operations on the data, integrating these capabilities into your mobile API endpoints.

Chapter 2: Setting up a Flask Development Environment

In the world of mobile app development, having a well-structured and efficient development environment is crucial for building robust API backends with the Flask framework. This chapter will guide you through the process of setting up a Flask development environment, ensuring that you have the necessary tools and configurations in place to start building and deploying your mobile API solutions.

Installing Flask and Related Dependencies

The foundation of a Flask development environment is, of course, the Flask framework itself. To get started, you'll need to install Flask and its associated dependencies. This can be accomplished using Python's built-in package manager, pip.

Open a terminal or command prompt and run the following command to install the latest version of Flask:

```
Copy
pip install flask
```

This command will download and install the Flask package, providing you with the core functionality required to start building web applications and APIs.

In addition to the core Flask framework, you may also need to install other packages and libraries that are commonly used in Flask-powered API development. Some of the most popular and useful dependencies include:

1. **Flask-SQLAlchemy**: A Flask extension that provides an Object-Relational Mapping (ORM) layer, simplifying the integration between Flask and various database engines.
2. **Flask-JWT-Extended**: A Flask extension that handles token-based authentication, making it easier to implement secure and scalable authentication mechanisms for your mobile APIs.
3. **Flask-Migrate**: A Flask extension that manages database schema migrations, allowing you to easily evolve your data models as your mobile app and API requirements change.
4. **Flask-RESTful**: A Flask extension that streamlines the process of building RESTful APIs, providing a set of abstractions and conventions to simplify API development.

You can install these dependencies using the same pip install command:

```
Copy
pip install flask-sqlalchemy flask-jwt-extended flask-migrate flask-restful
```

Depending on the specific needs of your mobile API project, you may also need to install additional packages and libraries. The beauty of Flask is its modular nature, allowing you to pick and choose the components that best fit your requirements.

Configuring a Development Workflow

With Flask and its dependencies installed, the next step is to set up a development workflow that will help you write, test, and deploy your mobile API solutions efficiently.

1. **Virtual Environments**: It is highly recommended to use a virtual environment to manage your project's Python dependencies. This

ensures that each project has its own isolated set of installed packages, preventing conflicts and version issues. Tools like virtualenv or pipenv can be used to create and manage virtual environments. To create a virtual environment using virtualenv, follow these steps:

```
Copy
# Install virtualenv if you haven't already
pip install virtualenv

# Create a new virtual environment
virtualenv venv

# Activate the virtual environment
# On Windows:
venv\Scripts\activate
# On macOS/Linux:
source venv/bin/activate
```

1. With the virtual environment activated, you can now install your project's dependencies without affecting your system's Python installation or other projects.
2. **Code Editors and IDEs**: Choosing a suitable code editor or Integrated Development Environment (IDE) can significantly enhance your productivity. Popular options for Flask development include PyCharm, Visual Studio Code, and the Sublime Text editor, all of which provide features like syntax highlighting, code completion, and integrated debugging capabilities. For example, if you're using Visual Studio Code, you can install the official Python extension, which provides a rich set of features for writing, testing, and debugging Flask applications.
3. **Version Control**: Implementing a version control system, such as Git, is crucial for managing the codebase of your Flask-powered mobile API. This allows you to track changes, collaborate with team members, and maintain a clear history of your project's development. To get

started with Git, you can install it from the official website (https://git-scm.com/downloads) and then initialize a new Git repository for your Flask project:

```
Copy
# Navigate to your project directory
cd /path/to/your/project

# Initialize a new Git repository
git init
```

1. Once the repository is set up, you can start committing your code changes and pushing them to a remote repository, such as GitHub, GitLab, or Bitbucket, for collaboration and backup purposes.
2. **Automated Testing**: Establishing a comprehensive testing suite is essential for ensuring the reliability and stability of your mobile API. Flask provides excellent support for writing unit tests, integration tests, and end-to-end tests using frameworks like unittest, pytest, or Postman. Here's an example of how you can set up a basic testing suite using the unittest framework:

```python
Copy
import unittest
from flask import Flask
from your_app import app, db, User

class TestUserModel(unittest.TestCase):
    def setUp(self):
        self.app = app
        self.app_context = self.
app.app_context()
```

CHAPTER 2: SETTING UP A FLASK DEVELOPMENT ENVIRONMENT

```
        self.app_context.push()
        db.create_all()

    def tearDown(self):
        db.session.remove()
        db.drop_all()
        self.app_context.pop()

    def test_create_user(self):
        user = User(name='John Doe', email='john.doe@example.com',
password_hash='secret')
        db.session.add(user)
        db.session.commit()
        self.assertEqual(User.query.count(), 1)

if __name__ == '__main__':
    unittest.main()
```

1. In this example, we're using the unittest framework to define a test case for the User model, which includes a test_create_user() method that verifies the ability to create a new user in the database. By writing and running these tests, you can ensure that your Flask-powered mobile API behaves as expected and catch regressions early in the development process.
2. **Continuous Integration and Deployment**: To streamline the process of building, testing, and deploying your Flask-powered mobile APIs, consider integrating your project with a Continuous Integration (CI) and Continuous Deployment (CD) platform, such as Travis CI, CircleCI, or GitHub Actions. These tools can automate the build, test, and deployment processes, ensuring that your mobile API is always up-to-date and ready for use. By setting up a CI/CD pipeline, you can:

- Automatically run your test suite on every commit or pull request, catching issues early.
- Build and package your Flask application for deployment.

- Deploy your API to various environments (e.g., development, staging, production) based on predefined triggers or manual approvals.

1. Here's an example of a basic .travis.yml configuration file that sets up a CI pipeline for a Flask project:

```yaml
Copy
language: python
python:
  - "3.9"
install:
  - pip install -r requirements.txt
script:
  - python -m unittest discover tests/
deploy:
  provider: heroku
  api_key:
    secure: YOUR_HEROKU_API_KEY
  app: your-flask-app
```

1. In this example, the CI pipeline will install the project's dependencies, run the test suite, and then deploy the application to Heroku when the tests pass.

By setting up a well-structured development workflow, you can ensure that your Flask-powered mobile API project is maintainable, scalable, and ready for production deployment. The tools and configurations discussed in this chapter will provide a solid foundation for your Flask development endeavors.

Chapter 3: Flask API Basics: Routing, Requests, and Responses

At the core of any Flask-powered mobile API is the ability to define routes, handle HTTP requests, and generate appropriate responses. In this chapter, we will explore the fundamental concepts and techniques for building robust and efficient API endpoints using Flask.

Defining API Endpoints with Flask Routes

The foundation of a Flask-powered API is the creation of routes, which map incoming HTTP requests to the corresponding Python functions that handle the logic and generate the responses. In Flask, you can define routes using the @app.route() decorator, which allows you to specify the URL patterns and the HTTP methods (GET, POST, PUT, DELETE) that the route should accept.

Here's a simple example of how to define a route for a mobile API endpoint:

```python
Copy
from flask import Flask, jsonify

app = Flask(__name__)

@app.route('/users',
 methods=['GET'])
def get_users():
    users = [
        {'id': 1, 'name': 'John Doe', 'email': 'john.doe@example.com'},
        {'id': 2, 'name': 'Jane Smith', 'email': 'jane.smith@example.com'},
    ]
    return jsonify(users)
```

In this example, the get_users() function is associated with the /users route and the GET HTTP method. When a client sends a GET request to the /users endpoint, Flask will automatically invoke the get_users() function and return the response as a JSON payload.

You can also define routes that accept parameters, which is particularly useful for building RESTful APIs. Here's an example:

```python
from flask import Flask, jsonify, request

app = Flask(__name__)

@app.route('/users/<int:user_id>'
, methods=['GET'])
def get_user(user_id):
    # Logic to retrieve a user by
ID from the database
    user = {'id': user_id, 'name':
'John Doe', 'email': 'john.doe@example.com'}
    return jsonify(user)
```

In this case, the get_user() function takes a user_id parameter, which is automatically extracted from the URL path and passed to the function. This allows you to build APIs that can retrieve, update, or delete specific resources based on their unique identifiers.

Handling HTTP Methods in Flask APIs

Flask's routing system allows you to specify which HTTP methods (GET, POST, PUT, DELETE) each endpoint should accept. This flexibility enables you to build RESTful APIs that follow the appropriate HTTP semantics for various CRUD (Create, Read, Update, Delete) operations.

Here's an example of how you can handle different HTTP methods for a user management API:

```python
from flask import Flask, jsonify, request

app = Flask(__name__)

@app.route('/users', methods=['GET', 'POST'])
def users():
    if request.method == 'GET':
```

CHAPTER 2: SETTING UP A FLASK DEVELOPMENT ENVIRONMENT

```
        users = [
            {'id': 1, 'name':
'John Doe', 'email': 'john.doe@example.com'},
            {'id': 2, 'name':
'Jane Smith', 'email':
'jane.smith@example.com'},
        ]
        return jsonify(users)
    elif request.method == 'POST':
        new_user = request.get_json()
        # Logic to create a new user
and store it in the database
        return jsonify(new_user), 201

@app.route('/users/<int:user_id>',
 methods=['GET', 'PUT', 'DELETE'])
def user(user_id):
    if request.method == 'GET':
        # Logic to retrieve a
specific user by ID
        user = {'id': user_id,
'name': 'John Doe', 'email':
'john.doe@example.com'}
        return jsonify(user)
    elif request.method == 'PUT':
        # Logic to update an
existing user by ID
        updated_user = request.get_json()
        return jsonify(updated_user)
    elif request.method == 'DELETE':
        # Logic to delete a user by ID
        return '', 204
```

In this example, the /users route handles both GET and POST requests, allowing clients to retrieve a list of users or create a new user, respectively. The /users/<int:user_id> route, on the other hand, handles GET, PUT, and DELETE requests, enabling clients to retrieve, update, and delete individual users by their unique identifier.

Parsing and Validating Request Data

When building mobile APIs, it's essential to handle incoming data from client requests effectively. Flask provides several ways to access and validate request data, ensuring that your API endpoints can process valid inputs and handle invalid ones gracefully.

One of the most common approaches is to use the request.get_json() method to retrieve the JSON-formatted data sent in the request body. Here's an example:

```python
Copy
from flask import Flask, jsonify, request
from flask_restful import Api, Resource, reqparse

app = Flask(__name__)
api = Api(app)

class UserResource(Resource):
    def post(self):
        parser = reqparse.RequestParser()
        parser.add_argument('name', type=str, required=True)
        parser.add_argument('email', type=str, required=True)
        args = parser.parse_args()

        # Logic to create a new user in the database using the validated input
        new_user = {'id': 1, 'name': args['name'], 'email': args['email']}
        return jsonify(new_user), 201

api.add_resource(UserResource, '/users')
```

In this example, we're using the flask_restful extension to define a UserResource class that handles the /users endpoint. The post() method uses the reqparse.RequestParser to define the expected parameters (name and email) and their validation rules (required string types). The parser.parse_args() call automatically validates the input data and returns a dictionary of the parsed arguments, which can then be used to create a new user in the database.

By validating the incoming request data, you can ensure that your mobile API endpoints are robust and can handle a variety of client inputs without failing or returning unexpected responses.

Returning Responses from Flask APIs

Once you've processed the incoming request and performed the necessary logic, it's time to return a response to the client. Flask provides several ways to generate and customize the responses, depending on the needs of your mobile API.

The most common approach is to use the jsonify() function, which automatically converts a Python dictionary or list into a JSON-formatted response:

```python
Copy
from flask import Flask, jsonify

app = Flask(__name__)

@app.route('/users/
<int:user_id>',
 methods=['GET'])
def get_user(user_id):
    user = {'id': user_id,
 'name': 'John Doe', 'email':
 'john.doe@example.com'}
    return jsonify(user)
```

In this example, the get_user() function returns a JSON response containing the user data.

In addition to jsonify(), you can also use the standard Flask.make_response() method to create custom responses, including setting status codes, headers, and even streaming data:

```python
Copy
from flask import Flask, make_response

app = Flask(__name__)

@app.route('/downloads/<filename>', methods=['GET'])
def download_file(filename):
    # Logic to retrieve the file from storage
    file_content = b'This is the content of the file.'

    response = make_response(file_content)
    response.headers.set('Content-Type', 'application/octet-stream')
    response.headers.set('Content-Disposition', 'attachment', filename=filename)
    return response
```

In this example, the download_file() function returns a custom response with a Content-Type header set to application/octet-stream and a Content-Disposition header set to attachment, indicating that the response should be treated as a file download.

By mastering the techniques for defining routes, handling HTTP methods, validating input, and returning responses, you can build robust and efficient mobile API backends using the Flask framework.

Chapter 4: Data Management with Flask-SQLAlchemy

One of the core responsibilities of a mobile API backend is the management and persistence of data. In the Flask ecosystem, the Flask-SQLAlchemy extension provides a powerful and intuitive way to integrate a database into your API, allowing you to define data models, perform CRUD (Create, Read, Update, Delete) operations, and establish relationships between entities.

Integrating a Database with Flask-SQLAlchemy

To get started with Flask-SQLAlchemy, you'll first need to install the extension and configure it within your Flask application:

```python
Copy
from flask import Flask
from flask_sqlalchemy import SQLAlchemy

app = Flask(__name__)
app.config['SQLALCHEMY_DATABASE_URI'] = 'sqlite:///database.db'
db = SQLAlchemy(app)
```

In this example, we're configuring the Flask-SQLAlchemy extension to use a SQLite database stored in a file named database.db. You can also configure Flask-SQLAlchemy to work with other database engines, such as PostgreSQL, MySQL, or Oracle, by modifying the SQLALCHEMY_DATABASE_URI setting accordingly.

Defining Data Models with Flask-SQLAlchemy

Once you've integrated the database, you can start defining your data models using the db.Model class provided by Flask-SQLAlchemy. These models represent the various entities and relationships in your mobile app's data schema.

Here's an example of a simple User model:

```python
Copy
from flask_sqlalchemy import SQLAlchemy

db = SQLAlchemy()

class User(db.Model):
    id = db.Column
(db.Integer, primary_key=
```

Chapter 3: Flask API Basics: Routing, Requests, and Responses

At the core of any Flask-powered mobile API is the ability to define routes, handle HTTP requests, and generate appropriate responses. In this chapter, we will explore the fundamental concepts and techniques for building robust and efficient API endpoints using Flask.

Defining API Endpoints with Flask Routes

The foundation of a Flask-powered API is the creation of routes, which map incoming HTTP requests to the corresponding Python functions that handle the logic and generate the responses. In Flask, you can define routes using the @app.route() decorator, which allows you to specify the URL patterns and the HTTP methods (GET, POST, PUT, DELETE) that the route should accept.

Here's a simple example of how to define a route for a mobile API endpoint:

```python
Copy
from flask import Flask, jsonify

app = Flask(__name__)

@app.route('/users', methods=['GET'])
def get_users():
```

CHAPTER 3: FLASK API BASICS: ROUTING, REQUESTS, AND...

```
    users = [
        {'id': 1, 'name':
'John Doe', 'email':
'john.doe@example.com'},
        {'id': 2, 'name':
'Jane Smith', 'email':
'jane.smith@example.com'},
    ]
    return jsonify(users)
```

In this example, the get_users() function is associated with the /users route and the GET HTTP method. When a client sends a GET request to the /users endpoint, Flask will automatically invoke the get_users() function and return the response as a JSON payload.

You can also define routes that accept parameters, which is particularly useful for building RESTful APIs. Here's an example:

```python
Copy
from flask import Flask, jsonify, request

app = Flask(__name__)

@app.route('/users/<int:user_id>',
 methods=['GET'])
def get_user(user_id):
    # Logic to retrieve a user
 by ID from the database
    user = {'id': user_id,
'name': 'John Doe', 'email':
'john.doe@example.com'}
    return jsonify(user)
```

In this case, the get_user() function takes a user_id parameter, which is automatically extracted from the URL path and passed to the function. This allows you to build APIs that can retrieve, update, or delete specific resources based on their unique identifiers.

Handling HTTP Methods in Flask APIs

Flask's routing system allows you to specify which HTTP methods (GET, POST, PUT, DELETE) each endpoint should accept. This flexibility enables you to build RESTful APIs that follow the appropriate HTTP semantics for various CRUD (Create, Read, Update, Delete) operations.

Here's an example of how you can handle different HTTP methods for a user management API:

```python
Copy
from flask import Flask, jsonify, request

app = Flask(__name__)

@app.route('/users', methods=['GET', 'POST'])
def users():
    if request.method == 'GET':
        users = [
            {'id': 1, 'name': 'John Doe', 'email': 'john.doe@example.com'},
            {'id': 2, 'name': 'Jane Smith', 'email': 'jane.smith@example.com'},
        ]
        return jsonify(users)
    elif request.method == 'POST':
        new_user = request.get_json()
        # Logic to create a new user and store it in the database
        return jsonify(new_user), 201

@app.route('/users/<int:user_id>', methods=['GET', 'PUT', 'DELETE'])
def user(user_id):
    if request.method == 'GET':
```

```
        # Logic to retrieve a
 specific user by ID
        user = {'id': user_id,
'name': 'John Doe', 'email':
'john.doe@example.com'}
return jsonify(user)
elif request.method == 'PUT':
# Logic to update an
 existing user by ID
updated_user = request.get_json()
return jsonify(updated_user)
elif request.method == 'DELETE':
# Logic to delete a user by ID
return '', 204
```

In this example, the /users route handles both GET and POST requests, allowing clients to retrieve a list of users or create a new user, respectively. The /users/<int:user_id> route, on the other hand, handles GET, PUT, and DELETE requests, enabling clients to retrieve, update, and delete individual users by their unique identifier.

Parsing and Validating Request Data

When building mobile APIs, it's essential to handle incoming data from client requests effectively. Flask provides several ways to access and validate request data, ensuring that your API endpoints can process valid inputs and handle invalid ones gracefully.

One of the most common approaches is to use the request.get_json() method to retrieve the JSON-formatted data sent in the request body. Here's an example:

```python
Copy
from flask import Flask,
jsonify, request
from flask_restful import
 Api, Resource, reqparse
```

```python
app = Flask(__name__)
api = Api(app)

class UserResource(Resource):
    def post(self):
        parser = reqparse.RequestParser()
        parser.add_argument('name', type=str, required=True)
        parser.add_argument('email', type=str, required=True)
        args = parser.parse_args()

        # Logic to create a new user in the database using the validated input
        new_user = {'id': 1, 'name': args['name'], 'email': args['email']}
        return jsonify(new_user), 201

api.add_resource(UserResource, '/users')
```

In this example, we're using the flask_restful extension to define a UserResource class that handles the /users endpoint. The post() method uses the reqparse.RequestParser to define the expected parameters (name and email) and their validation rules (required string types). The parser.parse_args() call automatically validates the input data and returns a dictionary of the parsed arguments, which can then be used to create a new user in the database.

By validating the incoming request data, you can ensure that your mobile API endpoints are robust and can handle a variety of client inputs without failing or returning unexpected responses.

Returning Responses from Flask APIs

Once you've processed the incoming request and performed the necessary logic, it's time to return a response to the client. Flask provides several ways to generate and customize the responses, depending on the needs of your mobile API.

The most common approach is to use the jsonify() function, which automatically converts a Python dictionary or list into a JSON-formatted response:

```python
Copy
from flask import Flask, jsonify

app = Flask(__name__)

@app.route('/users/
<int:user_id>', methods=['GET'])
def get_user(user_id):
    user = {'id': user_id,
 'name': 'John Doe', 'email':
 'john.doe@example.com'}
    return jsonify(user)
```

In this example, the get_user() function returns a JSON response containing the user data.

In addition to jsonify(), you can also use the standard Flask.make_response() method to create custom responses, including setting status codes, headers, and even streaming data:

```python
Copy
from flask import Flask, make_response

app = Flask(__name__)

@app.route('/downloads/
<filename>', methods=['GET'])
def download_file(filename):
    # Logic to retrieve the
 file from storage
    file_content = b
'This is the content of the file.'

    response = make
```

```
_response(file_content)
    response.headers.
set('Content-Type',
'application/octet-stream')
    response.headers.
set('Content-Disposition',
 'attachment', filename=filename)
    return response
```

In this example, the download_file() function returns a custom response with a Content-Type header set to application/octet-stream and a Content-Disposition header set to attachment, indicating that the response should be treated as a file download.

By mastering the techniques for defining routes, handling HTTP methods, validating input, and returning responses, you can build robust and efficient mobile API backends using the Flask framework.

Chapter 4: Data Management with Flask-SQLAlchemy

One of the core responsibilities of a mobile API backend is the management and persistence of data. In the Flask ecosystem, the Flask-SQLAlchemy extension provides a powerful and intuitive way to integrate a database into your API, allowing you to define data models, perform CRUD (Create, Read, Update, Delete) operations, and establish relationships between entities.

Integrating a Database with Flask-SQLAlchemy

To get started with Flask-SQLAlchemy, you'll first need to install the extension and configure it within your Flask application:

```python
Copy
from flask import Flask
from flask_sqlalchemy import SQLAlchemy

app = Flask(__name__)
app.config['SQLALCHEMY
_DATABASE_URI'] =
'sqlite:///database.db'
```

```
db = SQLAlchemy(app)
```

In this example, we're configuring the Flask-SQLAlchemy extension to use a SQLite database stored in a file named database.db. You can also configure Flask-SQLAlchemy to work with other database engines, such as PostgreSQL, MySQL, or Oracle, by modifying the SQLALCHEMY_DATABASE_URI setting accordingly.

Defining Data Models with Flask-SQLAlchemy

Once you've integrated the database, you can start defining your data models using the db.Model class provided by Flask-SQLAlchemy. These models represent the various entities and relationships in your mobile app's data schema.

Here's an example of a simple User model:

```python
Copy
from flask_sqlalchemy import SQLAlchemy

db = SQLAlchemy()

class User(db.Model):
    id = db.Column(db.Integer, primary_key=True)
    name = db.Column(db.String(50), nullable=False)
    email = db.Column(db.String(120), unique=True, nullable=False)
    password_hash = db.Column(db.String(100), nullable=False)

    def __repr__(self):
        return f'<User {self.name}>'
```

In this example, the User model has four columns: id, name, email, and password_hash. The db.Column() function is used to define the characteristics of each column, such as the data type, whether it's a primary key, and whether it's required (nullable).

The __repr__() method is a special method that returns a string representation of the model instance, which can be useful for debugging and logging purposes.

Performing CRUD Operations with Flask-SQLAlchemy

With the data models defined, you can now use Flask-SQLAlchemy to perform CRUD operations on the data, integrating these capabilities into your mobile API endpoints.

Here's an example of how you can create, retrieve, update, and delete users using the User model:

```python
Copy
from flask import Flask, jsonify, request
from flask_sqlalchemy import SQLAlchemy

app = Flask(__name__)
app.config['SQLALCHEMY_DATABASE_URI'] = 'sqlite:///database.db'
db = SQLAlchemy(app)

class User(db.Model):
    id = db.Column(db.Integer, primary_key=True)
    name = db.Column(db.String(50), nullable=False)
    email = db.Column(db.String(120), unique=True, nullable=False)
    password_hash = db.Column(db.String(100), nullable=False)

    def __repr__(self):
        return f'<User {self.name}>'

@app.route('/users',
```

```python
methods=['GET', 'POST'])
def users():
    if request.method == 'GET':
        users = User.query.all()
        return jsonify
([user.serialize() for user in users])
    elif request.method == 'POST':
        data = request.get_json()
new_user = User(name=data['name'], email=data['email'],
 password_hash=data
['password_hash'])
        db.session.add(new_user)
        db.session.commit()
        return jsonify
(new_user.serialize()), 201

@app.route('/users/
<int:user_id>', methods=
['GET', 'PUT', 'DELETE'])
def user(user_id):
    user = User.query.get(user_id)
    if request.method == 'GET':
        return jsonify
(user.serialize())
elif request.method == 'PUT':
data = request.get_json()
user.name = data['name']
user.email = data['email']
user.password_hash =
data['password_hash']
db.session.commit()
return jsonify
(user.serialize())
elif request.method == 'DELETE':
db.session.delete(user)
db.session.commit()
return '', 204

if __name__ == '__main__':
    app.run()
```

In this example, we've defined the User model and created two routes: /users and /users/<int:user_id>. The /users route handles GET and POST requests, allowing clients to retrieve a list of users or create a new user, respectively. The /users/<int:user_id> route, on the other hand, handles GET, PUT, and DELETE requests, enabling clients to retrieve, update, and delete individual users by their unique identifier.

The serialize() method in the User model is a custom method that converts the model instance into a dictionary, which can then be easily serialized to JSON and returned as the API response.

By using Flask-SQLAlchemy, you can seamlessly integrate a database into your mobile API, allowing you to persist and retrieve data as needed, without having to worry about the underlying database operations.

Chapter 5: Authentication and Authorization in Flask APIs

Secure authentication and authorization are crucial considerations when building mobile API backends. In this chapter, we'll explore how to implement these essential security features using Flask and related extensions.

Token-based Authentication with Flask-JWT-Extended

One of the most common and effective authentication mechanisms for mobile APIs is token-based authentication, which involves the client obtaining an authorization token (typically a JSON Web Token, or JWT) and including it in subsequent requests to the API. This approach is more secure than traditional session-based authentication, as it does not require maintaining server-side session state.

Flask-JWT-Extended is a popular extension that simplifies the implementation of token-based authentication in Flask applications. Here's an example of how to set it up:

```python
Copy
from flask import Flask, jsonify, request
from flask_jwt_extended import JWTManager, jwt_required, create_access_token
```

```python
app = Flask(__name__)
app.config['JWT_SECRET_KEY'] = 'your-secret-key'
jwt = JWTManager(app)

@app.route('/login', methods=['POST'])
def login():
    data = request.get_json()
    username = data.get('username')
    password = data.get('password')

    # Validate the username and password
    (e.g., against a database)
    if username == 'admin' and password == 'password':
        access_token = create_access_token(identity=username)
        return jsonify({'access_token': access_token}), 200
    else:
        return jsonify({'error': 'Invalid username or password'}), 401

@app.route('/protected', methods=['GET'])
@jwt_required()
def protected():
    # This route is only accessible to authenticated users
    user = get_jwt_identity()
    return jsonify({'message': f'Hello, {user}!'}), 200
```

In this example, we first set up the JWTManager with the Flask application and configure a secret key for signing the JWT tokens. Then, we create a /login endpoint that validates the user's credentials and, if successful, generates an access token using the create_access_token() function.

The @jwt_required() decorator is used to protect the /protected endpoint, ensuring that only authenticated users can access it. When a client includes a valid access token in the Authorization header of their request, Flask-JWT-Extended will automatically verify the token and provide the authenticated user's identity to the endpoint function.

Role-based Access Control (RBAC) in Flask APIs

In addition to user authentication, it's often necessary to implement fine-grained access control to ensure that users can only perform actions and access data that they're authorized to. One common approach is to use Role-based Access Control (RBAC), where users are assigned specific roles, and each role is granted permissions to perform certain actions.

Here's an example of how you can implement RBAC in a Flask API:

```python
Copy
from flask import Flask, jsonify, request
from flask_jwt_extended import JWTManager, jwt_required, get_jwt_identity
from functools import wraps

app = Flask(__name__)
app.config['JWT_SECRET_KEY'] = 'your-secret-key'
jwt = JWTManager(app)

# Define user roles and their permissions
ROLES = {
    'admin': ['create', 'read', 'update', 'delete'],
    'manager': ['read',
```

Chapter 4: Data Management with Flask-SQLAlchemy

One of the core responsibilities of a mobile API backend is the management and persistence of data. In the Flask ecosystem, the Flask-SQLAlchemy extension provides a powerful and intuitive way to integrate a database into your API, allowing you to define data models, perform CRUD (Create, Read, Update, Delete) operations, and establish relationships between entities.

Integrating a Database with Flask-SQLAlchemy

To get started with Flask-SQLAlchemy, you'll first need to install the extension and configure it within your Flask application:

```
python
Copy
from flask import Flask
from flask_sqlalchemy import SQLAlchemy

app = Flask(__name__)
app.config['SQLALCHEMY_DATABASE_URI'] = 'sqlite:///database.db'
db = SQLAlchemy(app)
```

In this example, we're configuring the Flask-SQLAlchemy extension to use a SQLite database stored in a file named database.db. You can also configure Flask-SQLAlchemy to work with other database engines, such as PostgreSQL, MySQL, or Oracle, by modifying the SQLALCHEMY_DATABASE_URI setting accordingly.

Defining Data Models with Flask-SQLAlchemy

Once you've integrated the database, you can start defining your data models using the db.Model class provided by Flask-SQLAlchemy. These models represent the various entities and relationships in your mobile app's data schema.

Here's an example of a simple User model:

```python
Copy
from flask_sqlalchemy import SQLAlchemy

db = SQLAlchemy()

class User(db.Model):
    id = db.Column(db.Integer, primary_key=True)
    name = db.Column(db.String(50), nullable=False)
    email = db.Column(db.String(120), unique=True, nullable=False)
    password_hash = db.Column(db.String(100), nullable=False)

    def __repr__(self):
        return f'<User {self.name}>'
```

In this example, the User model has four columns: id, name, email, and password_hash. The db.Column() function is used to define the characteristics of each column, such as the data type, whether it's a primary key, and whether it's required (nullable).

The __repr__() method is a special method that returns a string representation of the model instance, which can be useful for debugging and logging purposes.

Performing CRUD Operations with Flask-SQLAlchemy

CHAPTER 4: DATA MANAGEMENT WITH FLASK-SQLALCHEMY

With the data models defined, you can now use Flask-SQLAlchemy to perform CRUD operations on the data, integrating these capabilities into your mobile API endpoints.

Here's an example of how you can create, retrieve, update, and delete users using the User model:

```python
Copy
from flask import Flask, jsonify, request
from flask_sqlalchemy import SQLAlchemy

app = Flask(__name__)
app.config['SQLALCHEMY_DATABASE_URI'] = 'sqlite:///database.db'
db = SQLAlchemy(app)

class User(db.Model):
    id = db.Column(db.Integer, primary_key=True)
    name = db.Column(db.String(50), nullable=False)
    email = db.Column(db.String(120), unique=True, nullable=False)
    password_hash = db.Column(db.String(100), nullable=False)

    def __repr__(self):
        return f'<User {self.name}>'

    def serialize(self):
        return {
            'id': self.id,
            'name': self.name,
            'email': self.email
        }

@app.route('/users', methods=['GET', 'POST'])
```

```
def users():
    if request.method == 'GET':
users = User.query.all()
return jsonify([user.
serialize() for user in users])
elif request.method == 'POST':
data = request.get_json()
new_user = User
(name=data['name'],
email=data['email'], password_
hash=data['password_hash'])
        db.session.add(new_user)
        db.session.commit()
        return jsonify
(new_user.serialize()), 201

@app.route('/users/<int:user_id>',
 methods=['GET', 'PUT', 'DELETE'])
def user(user_id):
user = User.query.get(user_id)
if request.method == 'GET':
return jsonify(user.serialize())
    elif request.method == 'PUT':
data = request.get_json()
user.name = data['name']
user.email = data['email']
user.password_hash =
 data['password_hash']
db.session.commit()
return jsonify(user.serialize())
elif request.method == 'DELETE':
db.session.delete(user)
db.session.commit()
return '', 204

if __name__ == '__main__':
    app.run()
```

In this example, we've defined the User model and created two routes: /users and /users/<int:user_id>. The /users route handles GET and POST requests,

CHAPTER 4: DATA MANAGEMENT WITH FLASK-SQLALCHEMY

allowing clients to retrieve a list of users or create a new user, respectively. The /users/<int:user_id> route, on the other hand, handles GET, PUT, and DELETE requests, enabling clients to retrieve, update, and delete individual users by their unique identifier.

The serialize() method in the User model is a custom method that converts the model instance into a dictionary, which can then be easily serialized to JSON and returned as the API response.

By using Flask-SQLAlchemy, you can seamlessly integrate a database into your mobile API, allowing you to persist and retrieve data as needed, without having to worry about the underlying database operations.

Implementing Relationships Between Data Entities

In many mobile applications, the data models are not isolated but rather have relationships with each other. Flask-SQLAlchemy provides a straightforward way to define these relationships and leverage them in your API implementation.

Let's consider an example where a User model has a one-to-many relationship with a Post model, representing a user's blog posts:

```python
Copy
from flask_sqlalchemy import SQLAlchemy

db = SQLAlchemy()

class User(db.Model):
id = db.Column(db.
Integer, primary_key=True)
name = db.Column(db.
String(50), nullable=False)
email = db.Column(db.
String(120), unique=True,
 nullable=False)
password_hash = db.
Column(db.String(100),
 nullable=False)
    posts = db.relationship
```

```python
('Post', backref='author',
 lazy='dynamic')

def __repr__(self):
return f'<User {self.name}>'

def serialize(self):
return {
'id': self.id,
'name': self.name,
'email': self.email,
'posts': [post.serialize()
for post in self.posts]
        }

class Post(db.Model):
id = db.Column(db.Integer,
 primary_key=True)
    title = db.Column(db.
String(100), nullable=False)
content = db.
Column(db.Text, nullable=False)
user_id = db.Column(db.Integer,
db.ForeignKey('user.id'),
 nullable=False)

def __repr__(self):
return f'<Post {self.title}>'

def serialize(self):
return {
'id': self.id,
'title': self.title,
'content': self.content
        }
```

In this example, the User model has a posts attribute, which is a collection of Post objects associated with that user. The db.relationship() function defines the relationship, with the backref parameter specifying the name of the attribute that will be added to the Post model to access the associated

User instance.

The serialize() method in the User model now includes the serialized Post objects in the response, providing a way to retrieve the user's blog posts along with their basic information.

To create a new post and associate it with a user, you can do the following:

```python
Copy
@app.route('/users/<int:user_id>
/posts', methods=['POST'])
def create_post(user_id):
    data = request.get_json()
    user = User.query.get(user_id)
new_post = Post(title=data['title'], content=data['content'],
author=user)
    db.session.add(new_post)
    db.session.commit()
    return jsonify(new
post.serialize()), 201
```

In this example, we first retrieve the User instance by its ID, then create a new Post instance and associate it with the user by assigning the user object to the author attribute of the post. Finally, we add the new post to the database session and commit the changes.

By defining relationships between your data models, you can create more complex and interconnected APIs that better reflect the structure of your mobile app's data.

Advanced Database Operations with Flask-SQLAlchemy

While the basic CRUD operations are essential, Flask-SQLAlchemy provides a wealth of additional features and capabilities that can help you build more sophisticated and powerful mobile APIs.

1. **Querying and Filtering**: Flask-SQLAlchemy's query API allows you to perform complex queries and filtering on your data models. You can use methods like filter(), filter_by(), order_by(), and limit() to refine the data returned by your API endpoints.

```python
Copy
# Retrieve the 10 most recent
 posts by a specific user
recent_posts = user.posts.order_by
(Post.id.desc()).limit(10).all()
```

1. **Eager Loading and Relationships**: When working with related data models, you can use Flask-SQLAlchemy's support for eager loading to optimize database queries and reduce the number of network requests required by your mobile app.

```python
Copy
# Retrieve a user and their
 posts in a single query
user = User.query.options(db.
joinedload(User.posts)).
get(user_id)
```

1. **Transactions and Concurrency Control**: Flask-SQLAlchemy provides a straightforward way to manage database transactions, ensuring data integrity and consistency, especially when dealing with complex operations that involve multiple related entities.

```python
Copy
with db.session.begin_nested():
    new_user = User(name='John Doe', email='john.doe@example.com')
    db.session.add(new_user)
```

CHAPTER 4: DATA MANAGEMENT WITH FLASK-SQLALCHEMY

```
# Other database operations
```

1. **Database Migrations with Flask-Migrate**: As your mobile app evolves and its data requirements change, you'll need to manage database schema changes. The Flask-Migrate extension, built on top of Alembic, simplifies this process by generating and applying database migration scripts.

```
Copy
# Generate a new migration script
flask db migrate -m
"Add user profile picture"

# Apply the migration
flask db upgrade
```

1. **Database Caching and Performance Optimization**: For APIs that need to handle high volumes of traffic or large amounts of data, you can leverage caching strategies and other performance optimization techniques provided by Flask-SQLAlchemy and the underlying database engine.

By taking advantage of these advanced features, you can build mobile APIs that are not only functional but also scalable, efficient, and maintainable.

Conclusion

In this chapter, we've explored the core concepts and techniques for managing data in your Flask-powered mobile API backends using the Flask-SQLAlchemy extension. From integrating a database, defining data models, and performing CRUD operations to implementing relationships and advanced database features, you now have a solid foundation for building robust and flexible data management solutions for your mobile applications.

As you continue to develop your mobile APIs, remember to consider factors like performance, scalability, and maintainability, as they will be crucial in delivering a seamless and reliable experience to your mobile app users.

Chapter 5: Authentication and Authorization in Flask APIs

Secure authentication and authorization are crucial considerations when building mobile API backends. In this chapter, we'll explore how to implement these essential security features using Flask and related extensions.

Token-based Authentication with Flask-JWT-Extended

One of the most common and effective authentication mechanisms for mobile APIs is token-based authentication, which involves the client obtaining an authorization token (typically a JSON Web Token, or JWT) and including it in subsequent requests to the API. This approach is more secure than traditional session-based authentication, as it does not require maintaining server-side session state.

Flask-JWT-Extended is a popular extension that simplifies the implementation of token-based authentication in Flask applications. Here's an example of how to set it up:

```python
Copy
from flask import Flask, jsonify, request
from flask_jwt_extended import JWTManager, jwt_required, create_access_token
```

FLASK API FOR MOBILE APP DEVELOPMENT

```python
app = Flask(__name__)
app.config['JWT_SECRET_KEY']
= 'your-secret-key'
jwt = JWTManager(app)

@app.route('/login', methods=['POST'])
def login():
data = request.get_json()
username = data.get('username')
password = data.get('password')

# Validate the username
 and password (e.g.,
against a database)
\if username == 'admin'
 and password == 'password':
access_token = create_access_token
(identity=username)
\return jsonify
({'access_token': access_token}), 200
    else:
return jsonify
({'error': 'Invalid username
or password'}), 401

@app.route('/protected',
 methods=['GET'])
@jwt_required()
def protected():
    # This route is only
accessible to authenticated users
user = get_jwt_identity()
return jsonify
({'message': f'Hello, {user}!'}), 200
```

In this example, we first set up the JWTManager with the Flask application and configure a secret key for signing the JWT tokens. Then, we create a /login endpoint that validates the user's credentials and, if successful, generates an access token using the create_access_token() function.

CHAPTER 5: AUTHENTICATION AND AUTHORIZATION IN FLASK APIS

The @jwt_required() decorator is used to protect the /protected endpoint, ensuring that only authenticated users can access it. When a client includes a valid access token in the Authorization header of their request, Flask-JWT-Extended will automatically verify the token and provide the authenticated user's identity to the endpoint function.

Role-based Access Control (RBAC) in Flask APIs

In addition to user authentication, it's often necessary to implement fine-grained access control to ensure that users can only perform actions and access data that they're authorized to. One common approach is to use Role-based Access Control (RBAC), where users are assigned specific roles, and each role is granted permissions to perform certain actions.

Here's an example of how you can implement RBAC in a Flask API:

```python
Copy
from flask import Flask, jsonify, request
from flask_jwt_extended import JWTManager, jwt_required, get_jwt_identity
from functools import wraps

app = Flask(__name__)
app.config['JWT_SECRET_KEY'] = 'your-secret-key'
jwt = JWTManager(app)

# Define user roles and their permissions
ROLES = {
'admin': ['create',
'read', 'update', 'delete'],
'manager': ['read', 'update'],
'user': ['read']
}

def requires_role(role):
def decorator(func):
@wraps(func)
@jwt_required()
def wrapper(*args, **kwargs):
```

FLASK API FOR MOBILE APP DEVELOPMENT

```python
user_role = get_user_role
(get_jwt_identity())
if role in ROLES[user_role]:
return func(*args, **kwargs)
else:
return jsonify({'error':
'Forbidden'}), 403
return wrapper
return decorator

def get_user_role(username):
# Lookup the user's
 role in a database or
other authentication provider
if username == 'admin':
return 'admin'
elif username == 'manager':
return 'manager'
    else:
        return 'user'

@app.route('/users', methods=
['GET', 'POST'])
@requires_role('admin')
def users():
    if request.method == 'GET':
# Return a list of users
return jsonify([{'id': 1,
 'name': 'John Doe'},
{'id': 2, 'name': 'Jane Smith'}])
elif request.method == 'POST':
# Create a new user
data = request.get_json()
        # ...

@app.route('/users/<int:user_id>',
methods=['GET', 'PUT', 'DELETE'])
@requires_role('admin')
def user(user_id):
if request.method == 'GET':
```

CHAPTER 5: AUTHENTICATION AND AUTHORIZATION IN FLASK APIS

```python
# Return details of a specific user
return jsonify
({'id': user_id, 'name':
 'John Doe'})
elif request.method == 'PUT':
# Update a user
data = request.get_json()
        # ...
elif request.method == 'DELETE':
# Delete a user
        # ...

@app.route('/reports',
methods=['GET'])
@requires_role('manager')
def reports():
# Return some reports
return jsonify
([{'id': 1, 'title':
'Sales Report'},
{'id': 2, 'title':
'Marketing Report'}])
```

In this example, we define a ROLES dictionary that maps user roles to their corresponding permissions. The requires_role() decorator is used to protect the API endpoints, ensuring that only users with the appropriate role can access them.

The get_user_role() function is a placeholder for retrieving the user's role, which in a real-world application would likely involve querying a user database or an external authentication provider.

By using the @requires_role() decorator, we can easily protect our API endpoints and ensure that only authorized users can perform specific actions. In the example, the /users and /users/<int:user_id> endpoints are restricted to users with the 'admin' role, while the /reports endpoint is accessible to users with the 'manager' role.

Securing Sensitive Information and API Keys

In addition to authentication and authorization, it's crucial to properly secure sensitive information and API keys within your Flask-powered mobile API. This includes protecting things like database credentials, third-party service API keys, and any other confidential data that should not be exposed to clients or unauthorized users.

Here are some best practices for securing sensitive information in your Flask API:

1. **Environment Variables**: Instead of hardcoding sensitive information directly in your Flask application code, store them as environment variables. This ensures that the sensitive data is not committed to your code repository and can be easily managed and rotated as needed.

```python
Copy
import os

app.config['DB_USERNAME'] = os.getenv('DB_USERNAME')
app.config['DB_PASSWORD'] = os.getenv('DB_PASSWORD')
```

1. **Secure Configuration Management**: Use a secure configuration management tool, such as Hashicorp Vault or AWS Secrets Manager, to store and manage your sensitive information. These tools provide fine-grained access control, audit logging, and secure storage for your API keys and other secrets.
2. **API Key Management**: Implement a system for generating, distributing, and revoking API keys for your mobile app clients. This allows you to control access to your API and quickly respond to potential security breaches.

CHAPTER 5: AUTHENTICATION AND AUTHORIZATION IN FLASK APIS

```python
Copy
from flask import Flask, jsonify, request
from flask_apikey import APIKey

app = Flask(__name__)
api_key = APIKey(app)

@app.route('/api/data', methods=['GET'])
@api_key.required
def get_data():
    # Retrieve and return data
    return jsonify({'data': 'some sensitive information'})
```

1. In this example, we're using the Flask-APIKey extension to manage API keys and protect the /api/data endpoint, ensuring that only authorized clients can access the sensitive data.
2. **Secure Communication with HTTPS**: Ensure that all communication between your mobile app and the Flask API is encrypted using HTTPS. This protects the data in transit, including any sensitive information or API keys.
3. **Rotate Secrets Regularly**: Implement a process to regularly rotate your API keys, database credentials, and other sensitive information to minimize the risk of exposure.
4. **Logging and Monitoring**: Implement robust logging and monitoring solutions to track access to your API and detect any suspicious activity. This will help you quickly identify and respond to potential security breaches.

By following these best practices, you can ensure that your Flask-powered mobile API is both secure and compliant with industry standards and regulations, protecting your users' sensitive information and your own intellectual property.

Conclusion

In this chapter, we've explored the essential security features required for building robust and secure mobile API backends using Flask. From implementing token-based authentication with Flask-JWT-Extended to enforcing role-based access control (RBAC), you now have the tools and knowledge to build mobile APIs that can effectively manage user authentication and authorization.

Additionally, we've discussed various techniques for securing sensitive information and API keys, ensuring that your mobile API is protected from unauthorized access and data breaches. By incorporating these security measures into your Flask-powered mobile API, you can provide a reliable and trustworthy service to your mobile app users.

As you continue to develop your mobile API solutions, remember to stay up-to-date with the latest security best practices and industry standards to maintain the highest levels of security and compliance.

Part II: Building Production-Ready Flask APIs Chapter 6: Designing Scalable and Performant API Architectures

As mobile app usage continues to grow, the demand for high-performing and scalable API backends has become increasingly critical. In this chapter, we'll explore strategies and techniques for building Flask-powered APIs that can handle large data volumes, concurrent requests, and ever-increasing traffic loads.

Strategies for Improving API Performance

1. **Caching**: Caching is one of the most effective ways to improve the performance of your Flask API. By caching frequently accessed data, you can reduce the number of database queries and processing required for each request, resulting in faster response times for your mobile app users. Flask-Caching is a popular extension that simplifies the implementation of caching in your Flask API. Here's an example of how you can use it:

```python
Copy
from flask import Flask
from flask_caching import Cache
```

FLASK API FOR MOBILE APP DEVELOPMENT

```python
app = Flask(__name__)
cache = Cache(app, config={
    'CACHE_TYPE': 'redis',
    'CACHE_REDIS_HOST': 'redis://localhost:6379'
})

@app.route('/users/<int:user_id>',
 methods=['GET'])
@cache.memoize(timeout=3600)
# Cache the response for 1 hour
def get_user(user_id):
    # Retrieve user data from the database
    user = User.query.get(user_id)
    return jsonify(user.serialize())
```

1. In this example, we're using the Redis caching backend provided by Flask-Caching to cache the response of the /users/<int:user_id> endpoint for 1 hour. This means that subsequent requests for the same user within that time frame will be served from the cache, rather than querying the database.

2. **Asynchronous Programming**: For long-running or resource-intensive operations, you can leverage asynchronous programming techniques to offload the work to a separate thread or process, allowing your Flask API to continue serving other requests without delay. Flask provides built-in support for asynchronous programming through the use of the async and await keywords. You can also use third-party libraries like Celery or RQ to implement asynchronous task queues and background workers.

```
python
Copy
from flask import Flask
from celery import Celery
```

```
app = Flask(__name__)
app.config.from_object('config')

celery = Celery(app.name, broker=
app.config['CELERY_BROKER_URL'])
celery.conf.update(app.config)

@app.route('/process_image',
 methods=['POST'])
def process_image():
    data = request.get_json()
    process_image_task.delay
(data['image_url'])
    return jsonify({'message':
'Image processing job started'}), 202

@celery.task
def process_image_task(image_url):
    # Perform the image processing
 logic in the background
    # ...
```

1. In this example, we're using Celery to offload the image processing logic to a background worker. When the /process_image endpoint is called, it immediately returns a 202 Accepted response, and the actual processing is handled by the process_image_task Celery worker in the background.
2. **Database Optimization**: Optimizing your database queries and schema can also have a significant impact on the performance of your Flask API. Techniques like indexing, denormalization, and schema design can help reduce the load on your database and improve response times. Additionally, you can explore the use of specialized databases, such as Redis or Memcached, for caching and storing frequently accessed data, reducing the load on your primary database.
3. **Content Delivery Network (CDN)**: If your Flask API is serving static assets, such as images, CSS, or JavaScript files, you can leverage a Content

Delivery Network (CDN) to improve the delivery of these resources. A CDN can cache and serve the static content from geographically distributed servers, reducing the load on your Flask API and improving the overall responsiveness of your mobile app.

Handling Large Data Volumes and Concurrent Requests

As your mobile user base grows, your Flask API will need to handle increasing amounts of data and a higher number of concurrent requests. Here are some strategies to address these challenges:

1. **Pagination and Cursors**: Implement pagination and cursor-based pagination mechanisms in your API endpoints to limit the amount of data returned per request. This helps reduce the load on your database and improve the responsiveness of your API.

```python
Copy
from flask import Flask, jsonify, request
from flask_sqlalchemy import SQLAlchemy

app = Flask(__name__)
db = SQLAlchemy(app)

class Post(db.Model):
    id = db.Column(db.Integer,
     primary_key=True)
    title = db.Column(db.String
    (100), nullable=False)
    content = db.Column(db.
    Text, nullable=False)

@app.route('/posts',
 methods=['GET'])
def get_posts():
    page = request.args.
```

```
get('page', 1, type=int)
    per_page = request.args.
get('per_page', 10, type=int)
    posts = Post.query.paginate
(page=page, per_page=per_page)
    return jsonify([post.serialize()
 for post in posts.items])
```

1. In this example, the /posts endpoint supports pagination through the page and per_page query parameters. This allows the mobile app to request a specific page of results, reducing the amount of data transferred in each response.
2. **Asynchronous Processing and Task Queues**: For long-running or resource-intensive operations, use asynchronous processing and task queues (as discussed in the previous section) to offload the work to background workers. This ensures that your Flask API can continue serving other requests without delay, even when handling large data volumes or complex tasks.
3. **Database Scalability**: Ensure that your database can handle the growing data volume and concurrency requirements of your mobile API. This may involve scaling vertically (upgrading hardware resources) or horizontally (sharding or partitioning data, using a distributed database system). Additionally, consider using a database-as-a-service (DBaaS) offering, which can provide automatic scaling, high availability, and other operational benefits, allowing you to focus on building your API rather than managing the database infrastructure.
4. **Load Balancing and Horizontal Scaling**: As the number of concurrent requests to your Flask API increases, you'll need to implement load balancing and horizontal scaling to distribute the load across multiple instances of your application. You can use a load balancer, such as Nginx or Amazon Elastic Load Balancing (ELB), to distribute incoming requests across multiple Flask API instances, ensuring that your system can handle the increased traffic. Additionally, you can leverage

container orchestration platforms like Docker Swarm or Kubernetes to automatically scale your Flask API instances up or down based on the incoming load.

Designing for Scalability and Load Balancing

Designing your Flask API architecture with scalability in mind is crucial for handling future growth and ensuring that your mobile app users have a consistently positive experience.

1. **Microservices Architecture**: Consider adopting a microservices architecture, where your Flask API is composed of smaller, independent services that can be scaled and deployed independently. This approach promotes modularity, flexibility, and easier scaling compared to a monolithic architecture.

```python
Copy
# Example of a microservices-based Flask API
from flask import Flask, jsonify
from flask_sqlalchemy import SQLAlchemy

app = Flask(__name__)
db = SQLAlchemy(app)

class User(db.Model):
    id = db.Column(db.Integer, primary_key=True)
    name = db.Column(db.String(50), nullable=False)
    email = db.Column(db.String(120), unique=True, nullable=False)

@app.route('/users', methods=['GET'])
def get_users():
```

```
users = User.query.all()
return jsonify([user.serialize
() for user in users])

if __name__ == '__main__':
    app.run()
```

1. **Stateless API Design**: Ensure that your Flask API is stateless, meaning that each request can be handled independently without relying on server-side session data or state. This allows you to easily scale your API horizontally by adding more instances behind a load balancer, as the individual instances don't need to coordinate or share state.
2. **Caching and Content Delivery Network (CDN)**: Leverage caching and CDN strategies (as discussed earlier) to offload the delivery of static content and frequently accessed data from your Flask API. This reduces the load on your API servers and allows you to scale your compute resources more efficiently.
3. **Asynchronous Processing and Message Queues**: Implement asynchronous processing and message queues to handle long-running or resource-intensive tasks. This ensures that your Flask API can continue serving other requests while the background tasks are being processed, improving the overall responsiveness and scalability of your system.
4. **Monitoring and Autoscaling**: Implement robust monitoring and logging solutions to track the performance and resource utilization of your Flask API. This data can be used to trigger autoscaling mechanisms, such as those provided by cloud platforms like AWS or Google Cloud, to automatically scale your API instances up or down based on the incoming load.
5. **Database Scalability**: Ensure that your database can scale to handle the growing data and concurrency requirements of your mobile API. This may involve techniques like sharding, partitioning, or using a distributed database system. Additionally, consider using a database-as-a-service (DBaaS) offering, which can provide automatic scaling, high availability,

and other operational benefits, allowing you to focus on building your API rather than managing the database infrastructure.

By incorporating these design principles and strategies into your Flask API architecture, you can build production-ready APIs that are scalable, performant, and capable of handling the demands of your growing mobile user base.

Chapter 7: Versioning and Evolving Flask APIs

As your mobile app and its backend requirements evolve over time, it's crucial to have a well-defined strategy for versioning and evolving your Flask API. This ensures that you can introduce new features and improvements without breaking existing mobile app integrations.

API Versioning Strategies

There are several approaches to versioning your Flask API, each with its own advantages and trade-offs. The most common strategies include:

1. **URL-based Versioning**: In this approach, the API version is included in the URL path, like /v1/users or /v2/users.

```python
Copy
from flask import Flask, jsonify

app = Flask(__name__)

@app.route('/v1/users', methods=['GET'])
def get_users_v1():
# Version 1 implementation
return jsonify([{'id': 1
, 'name': 'John Doe'}])

@app.route('/v2/users',
 methods=['GET'])
```

```python
def get_users_v2():
    # Version 2 implementation
    return jsonify([{'id': 1,
 'name': 'John Doe',
'email': 'john.doe@example.com'}])
```

1. This approach is simple to implement and understand, but it can lead to longer and less intuitive URLs.
2. **Header-based Versioning**: In this approach, the API version is included in the request headers, such as X-API-Version: 1.

```python
Copy
from flask import Flask, jsonify, request

app = Flask(__name__)

@app.route('/users',
methods=['GET'])
def get_users():
api_version = request.headers.
get('X-API-Version', '1')
if api_version == '1':
# Version 1 implementation
return jsonify([{'id': 1,
'name': 'John Doe'}])
elif api_version == '2':
# Version 2 implementation
return jsonify([{'id': 1,
 'name': 'John Doe', 'email':
 'john.doe@example.com'}])
else:
return jsonify({'error':
'Unsupported API version'}), 400
```

1. This approach keeps the URL structure cleaner, but it requires clients to include the version information in the request headers.
2. **Content Negotiation**: In this approach, the API version is specified in the Accept header of the request, using a custom media type that includes the version information, such as application/vnd.example.v1+json.

```python
Copy
from flask import Flask, jsonify, request

app = Flask(__name__)

@app.route('/users', methods=['GET'])
def get_users():
    accept_header = request.headers.get('Accept')
    if accept_header == 'application/vnd.example.v1+json':
        # Version 1 implementation
        return jsonify([{'id': 1, 'name': 'John Doe'}])
    elif accept_header == 'application/vnd.example.v2+json':
        # Version 2 implementation
        return jsonify([{'id': 1, 'name': 'John Doe', 'email': 'john.doe@example.com'}])
    else:
        return jsonify({'error': 'Unsupported media type'}), 406
```

1. This approach is more flexible and can allow for more complex versioning schemes, but it requires clients to be more aware of the versioning mechanism.

Regardless of the versioning strategy you choose, it's essential to maintain consistent and clear documentation for your API versioning scheme, ensuring that mobile app developers can easily integrate with your Flask API.

Deprecating and Upgrading API Versions

As your Flask API evolves, you'll need to deprecate old versions and introduce new ones. Here are some best practices for managing this process:

1. **Deprecation Notice**: When you decide to deprecate an API version, provide clear and prominent notices to your mobile app developers, informing them of the deprecation timeline and the recommended actions they should take.

```python
Copy
from flask import Flask, jsonify, request

app = Flask(__name__)

@app.route('/v1/users',
 methods=['GET'])
def get_users_v1():
    # Version 1 implementation
    return jsonify([{'id': 1,
'name': 'John Doe'}])

@app.route('/v2/users',
 methods=['GET'])
def get_users_v2():
    # Version 2 implementation
    return jsonify([{'id': 1,
'name': 'John Doe',
'email': 'john.doe@example.com'}])

@app.route('/users', methods=['GET'])
def get_users():
# Deprecation notice
```

```
if request.headers.
get('X-API-Version') == '1':
return jsonify({'error':
'Version 1 of the API is deprecated.
Please upgrade to version 2.'}), 410
# Version 2 implementation
return get_users_v2()
```

1. In this example, the /users endpoint checks if the client is using the deprecated version 1 API and returns a 410 Gone response with a deprecation notice.
2. **Gradual Deprecation**: Instead of abruptly removing an API version, consider a gradual deprecation process. This gives mobile app developers more time to migrate their integrations to the newer version of your Flask API. For example, you could start by marking the old version as deprecated, then maintain it for a period of time before eventually removing it completely.
3. **Versioning Conventions**: Establish a clear versioning convention for your Flask API, such as using semantic versioning (e.g., 1.2.3) or a simple numeric versioning scheme (e.g., v1, v2). This makes it easier for mobile app developers to understand the scope of changes between versions.
4. **Backwards Compatibility**: When introducing a new version of your Flask API, strive to maintain backwards compatibility as much as possible. This means preserving existing endpoints, data formats, and behavior, unless there is a compelling reason to make breaking changes. Backwards compatibility ensures a smoother transition for mobile app developers, reducing the effort required to migrate their applications to the new API version.
5. **Version Migration Guides**: Provide clear and comprehensive migration guides to assist mobile app developers in upgrading their integrations from one version of your Flask API to the next. These guides should detail the changes, deprecations, and any necessary steps for a successful migration.

By following these best practices for API versioning and evolution, you can ensure a smooth and seamless transition for your mobile app developers, enabling them to integrate with your Flask-powered API with confidence and ease.

Conclusion

In this chapter, we've explored the key considerations and strategies for building production-ready Flask APIs that are scalable, performant, and able to evolve over time.

Chapter 7: Versioning and Evolving Flask APIs

As your mobile app and its backend requirements evolve over time, it's crucial to have a well-defined strategy for versioning and evolving your Flask API. This ensures that you can introduce new features and improvements without breaking existing mobile app integrations.

API Versioning Strategies

There are several approaches to versioning your Flask API, each with its own advantages and trade-offs. The most common strategies include:

1. **URL-based Versioning**: In this approach, the API version is included in the URL path, like /v1/users or /v2/users.

```python
Copy
from flask import Flask, jsonify

app = Flask(__name__)

@app.route('/v1/users', methods=['GET'])
def get_users_v1():
    # Version 1 implementation
    return jsonify([{'id':
```

CHAPTER 7: VERSIONING AND EVOLVING FLASK APIS

```
1, 'name': 'John Doe'}])

@app.route('/v2/users',
 methods=['GET'])
def get_users_v2():
    # Version 2 implementation
    return jsonify([{'id': 1
, 'name': 'John Doe', 'email':
 'john.doe@example.com'}])
```

1. This approach is simple to implement and understand, but it can lead to longer and less intuitive URLs.
2. **Header-based Versioning**: In this approach, the API version is included in the request headers, such as X-API-Version: 1.

```python
Copy
from flask import Flask, jsonify, request

app = Flask(__name__)

@app.route('/users', methods=['GET'])
def get_users():
api_version = request.headers.
get('X-API-Version', '1')
if api_version == '1':
# Version 1 implementation
return jsonify([{'id': 1,
'name': 'John Doe'}])
elif api_version == '2':
# Version 2 implementation
return jsonify
([{'id': 1, 'name': 'John Doe',
'email': 'john.doe@example.com'}])
    else:
```

```
return jsonify({'error':
 'Unsupported API version'}), 400
```

1. This approach keeps the URL structure cleaner, but it requires clients to include the version information in the request headers.
2. **Content Negotiation**: In this approach, the API version is specified in the Accept header of the request, using a custom media type that includes the version information, such as application/vnd.example.v1+json.

```python
Copy
from flask import Flask, jsonify, request

app = Flask(__name__)

@app.route('/users', methods=['GET'])
def get_users():
    accept_header = request.headers.get('Accept')
    if accept_header == 'application/vnd.example.v1+json':
       # Version 1 implementation
       return jsonify([{'id': 1, 'name': 'John Doe'}])
    elif accept_header == 'application/vnd.example.v2+json':
       # Version 2 implementation
       return jsonify([{'id': 1, 'name': 'John Doe', 'email': 'john.doe@example.com'}])
    else:
       return jsonify({'error': 'Unsupported media type'}), 406
```

1. This approach is more flexible and can allow for more complex version-

CHAPTER 7: VERSIONING AND EVOLVING FLASK APIS

ing schemes, but it requires clients to be more aware of the versioning mechanism.

Regardless of the versioning strategy you choose, it's essential to maintain consistent and clear documentation for your API versioning scheme, ensuring that mobile app developers can easily integrate with your Flask API.

Deprecating and Upgrading API Versions

As your Flask API evolves, you'll need to deprecate old versions and introduce new ones. Here are some best practices for managing this process:

1. **Deprecation Notice**: When you decide to deprecate an API version, provide clear and prominent notices to your mobile app developers, informing them of the deprecation timeline and the recommended actions they should take.

```python
Copy
from flask import Flask, jsonify, request

app = Flask(__name__)

@app.route('/v1/users', methods=['GET'])
def get_users_v1():
# Version 1 implementation
return jsonify
([{'id': 1, 'name': 'John Doe'}])

@app.route('/v2/users', methods=['GET'])
def get_users_v2():
# Version 2 implementation
return jsonify([{'id': 1,
'name': 'John Doe', 'email':
'john.doe@example.com'}])

@app.route('/users',
```

```
methods=['GET'])
def get_users():
    # Deprecation notice
    if request.headers.
get('X-API-Version') == '1':
return jsonify({'error':
'Version 1 of the API is deprecated.
Please upgrade to version 2.'}), 410
    # Version 2 implementation
    return get_users_v2()
```

1. In this example, the /users endpoint checks if the client is using the deprecated version 1 API and returns a 410 Gone response with a deprecation notice.
2. **Gradual Deprecation**: Instead of abruptly removing an API version, consider a gradual deprecation process. This gives mobile app developers more time to migrate their integrations to the newer version of your Flask API. For example, you could start by marking the old version as deprecated, then maintain it for a period of time before eventually removing it completely.
3. **Versioning Conventions**: Establish a clear versioning convention for your Flask API, such as using semantic versioning (e.g., 1.2.3) or a simple numeric versioning scheme (e.g., v1, v2). This makes it easier for mobile app developers to understand the scope of changes between versions.
4. **Backwards Compatibility**: When introducing a new version of your Flask API, strive to maintain backwards compatibility as much as possible. This means preserving existing endpoints, data formats, and behavior, unless there is a compelling reason to make breaking changes. Backwards compatibility ensures a smoother transition for mobile app developers, reducing the effort required to migrate their applications to the new API version.
5. **Version Migration Guides**: Provide clear and comprehensive migration guides to assist mobile app developers in upgrading their

CHAPTER 7: VERSIONING AND EVOLVING FLASK APIS

integrations from one version of your Flask API to the next. These guides should detail the changes, deprecations, and any necessary steps for a successful migration.

By following these best practices for API versioning and evolution, you can ensure a smooth and seamless transition for your mobile app developers, enabling them to integrate with your Flask-powered API with confidence and ease.

Upgrade Planning and Migration Considerations

When planning to upgrade your Flask API to a newer version, there are several key factors to consider to ensure a successful migration for your mobile app integrations.

1. **Impact Assessment**: Thoroughly analyze the changes and improvements introduced in the new API version, and assess the potential impact on your existing mobile app integrations. This includes identifying any breaking changes, deprecated features, and new functionality that may require updates to the mobile app. Engage with your mobile app development teams early in the process to understand their integration strategies and timeline, so you can align the API upgrade plans accordingly.

2. **Deprecation Timeline**: Establish a clear deprecation timeline for the old API version, and communicate it to your mobile app developers well in advance. This gives them ample time to plan and execute the migration to the new API version. Consider a gradual deprecation approach, where you first mark the old version as deprecated, maintain it for a certain period, and then completely remove it. This allows for a smoother transition and reduces the risk of disrupting existing mobile app integrations.

3. **Versioning and Compatibility**: Ensure that your versioning strategy, as discussed in the previous section, is well-defined and consistently applied across your API. This helps mobile app developers understand the scope of changes between versions and plan their migration accordingly. Additionally, strive to maintain backwards compatibility as much

as possible, preserving existing endpoints, data formats, and behavior, unless there are compelling reasons to make breaking changes. This reduces the effort required for mobile app developers to upgrade their integrations.

4. **Migration Guides and Documentation**: Provide clear and comprehensive migration guides to assist your mobile app developers in upgrading their integrations from one version of your Flask API to the next. These guides should detail the changes, deprecations, and any necessary steps for a successful migration. Ensure that your API documentation is up-to-date and reflects the changes introduced in the new version, making it easy for mobile app developers to understand and adopt the upgraded API.

5. **Phased Rollout and Canary Releases**: Consider a phased rollout approach, where you gradually introduce the new API version to a subset of your mobile app users before a full-scale deployment. This allows you to gather feedback, identify and address any issues, and ensure a smooth transition for the broader user base. Leverage techniques like Canary releases, where you gradually increase the percentage of users accessing the new API version, as a way to validate the upgrade and mitigate the risk of disrupting your mobile app integrations.

6. **Monitoring and Feedback Mechanisms**: Implement robust monitoring and logging solutions to track the usage and performance of your upgraded Flask API. This includes monitoring for any issues or regressions that may arise during the migration process. Establish clear communication channels and feedback mechanisms to gather input from your mobile app developers, allowing you to address any concerns or challenges they encounter during the upgrade process.

By carefully planning and executing the upgrade process, considering the impact on your mobile app integrations, and providing comprehensive migration support, you can ensure a smooth and successful transition to the new version of your Flask API.

Conclusion

In this chapter, we've explored the key considerations and strategies for versioning and evolving your Flask-powered API to meet the changing needs of your mobile app ecosystem.

From implementing various versioning strategies, such as URL-based, header-based, and content negotiation, to effectively deprecating old versions and maintaining backwards compatibility, you now have the knowledge to manage the lifecycle of your Flask API and ensure a seamless migration experience for your mobile app developers.

By following best practices like establishing clear versioning conventions, providing deprecation notices and migration guides, and planning for a phased rollout, you can build production-ready Flask APIs that can evolve over time without disrupting your existing mobile app integrations.

As you continue to develop and enhance your Flask-powered API, remember to prioritize communication, collaboration, and transparency with your mobile app development teams. This will help foster a smooth and collaborative ecosystem, where your API and mobile apps can jointly evolve to provide the best possible experience for your users.

Chapter 8: Integrating Flask APIs with Mobile Frameworks

As mobile app development continues to evolve, the need for seamless integration between the backend API and the frontend mobile frameworks has become increasingly important. In this chapter, we will explore the best practices and strategies for connecting your Flask-powered APIs with popular mobile development frameworks, such as React Native, Flutter, and native Android/iOS.

Connecting Flask Backends with React Native, Flutter, and Native Android/iOS

One of the key advantages of using Flask for your mobile API backend is its flexibility and compatibility with a wide range of frontend technologies. Whether your mobile app is built using React Native, Flutter, or native Android/iOS, you can effortlessly integrate your Flask API to power the data and functionality required by your mobile application.

1. **React Native Integration**: React Native is a popular framework for building cross-platform mobile applications using the React JavaScript library. Integrating a Flask API with a React Native app is straightforward, as both technologies share a common language (JavaScript/TypeScript) and can communicate seamlessly over HTTP. Here's an example of how you might integrate a Flask API with a React Native app:

CHAPTER 8: INTEGRATING FLASK APIS WITH MOBILE FRAMEWORKS

```javascript
Copy
// React Native component
import React, { useState, useEffect } from 'react';
import axios from 'axios';

const UserList = () => {
const [users, setUsers] =
 useState([]);

useEffect(() => {
const fetchUsers = async () => {
try {
const response = await
 axios.get('/api/users');
setUsers(response.data);
} catch (error) {
console.error
('Error fetching users:', error);
      }
    };
    fetchUsers();
  }, []);

  return (
    <View>
{users.map((user) => (
<Text key={user.id}>
{user.name}</Text>
      ))}
    </View>
  );
};
```

1. **Flutter Integration**: Flutter is a cross-platform mobile development framework created by Google, which uses the Dart programming language. Integrating a Flask API with a Flutter app is similar to the

79

React Native approach, as both platforms can communicate with APIs over HTTP.

```dart
// Flutter widget
import 'package:flutter/material.dart';
import 'package:http/http.dart' as http;
import 'dart:convert';

class UserList extends StatefulWidget {
@override
_UserListState createState()
 => _UserListState();
}

class _UserListState extends State<UserList> {
List<dynamic> users = [];

@override
void initState() {
super.initState();
_fetchUsers();
  }

Future<void> _fetchUsers() async {
final response = await http.get('/api/users');
if (response.statusCode == 200) {
setState(() {
users = json.decode(response.body);
      });
} else {
print('Error fetching users: ${response.statusCode}');
```

CHAPTER 8: INTEGRATING FLASK APIS WITH MOBILE FRAMEWORKS

```
    }
  }

  @override
  Widget build(BuildContext context) {
return ListView.builder(
itemCount: users.length,
itemBuilder: (context, index) {
final user = users[index];
return ListTile(
title: Text(user['name']),
        );
      },
    );
  }
}
```

1. **Native Android/iOS Integration**: For mobile apps built using native Android (Java/Kotlin) or iOS (Swift/Objective-C) technologies, integrating with a Flask API is typically done through standard HTTP client libraries provided by the respective platforms.

```kotlin
Copy
// Android example (Kotlin)
import com.android.volley.Request
import com.android.volley.RequestQueue
import com.android.volley.
toolbox.JsonArrayRequest
import com.android.
volley.toolbox.Volley

class UserListFragment : Fragment() {
private lateinit var requestQueue:
RequestQueue
private val users =
```

```kotlin
mutableListOf<User>()

override fun onViewCreated
(view: View, s
avedInstanceState: Bundle?) {
super.onViewCreated
(view, savedInstanceState)
requestQueue = Volley.
newRequestQueue(requireContext())
fetchUsers()
  }

  private fun fetchUsers() {
val url = "/api/users"
val request = JsonArrayRequest(
Request.Method.GET, url, null,
{ response ->
users.clear()
for (i in 0 until response.length()) {
val user = User(
response.getJSONObject
(i).getString("name")
          )
users.add(user)
        }
// Update the UI with the fetched users
      },
      { error -> Log.e
("UserListFragment",
 "Error fetching users: $error") }
    )
requestQueue.add(request)
  }
}
```

swift
Copy
```swift
// iOS example (Swift)
import UIKit

class UserListViewController:
```

CHAPTER 8: INTEGRATING FLASK APIS WITH MOBILE FRAMEWORKS

```
UITableViewController {
  private var users: [User] = []

  override func viewDidLoad() {
    super.viewDidLoad()
    fetchUsers()
  }

  private func fetchUsers() {
guard let url = URL(string:
"/api/users") else { return }
URLSession.shared.dataTask
(with: url) { (data, response, error) in
if let error = error {
print("Error fetching users: \(error)")
return
      }
if let data = data {
self.users = try? JSONDecoder().
decode([User].self, from: data)
DispatchQueue.main.async {
self.tableView.reloadData()
        }
      }
    }.resume()
  }

  // TableView data source and delegate methods
}
```

In these examples, we demonstrate how to fetch data from a Flask API using the respective HTTP client libraries available in React Native, Flutter, and native Android/iOS development. The key aspects are making an HTTP GET request to the API endpoint and then handling the response to update the user interface accordingly.

Best Practices for API Integration and Data Synchronization

When integrating your Flask API with mobile frameworks, there are several best practices to consider to ensure a seamless and efficient integration:

1. **API Design and Documentation**: Ensure that your Flask API is designed with mobile app integration in mind. This includes providing clear and comprehensive documentation, following RESTful principles, and using appropriate HTTP status codes and error handling.
2. **Consistent Data Formats**: Adopt a consistent data format, such as JSON, for your API responses. This simplifies the parsing and handling of data on the mobile app side, reducing the integration complexity.
3. **Pagination and Cursors**: Implement pagination and cursor-based mechanisms in your Flask API to limit the amount of data returned per request. This helps reduce the load on your mobile app and improve the overall user experience.
4. **Authentication and Authorization**: Leverage the authentication and authorization mechanisms you've implemented in your Flask API (as discussed in the previous chapter) to secure the integration with your mobile app. This ensures that only authorized users can access the appropriate data and functionality.
5. **Error Handling and Retries**: Ensure that your Flask API provides clear and informative error messages, and handle failures gracefully. On the mobile app side, implement robust error handling and retry mechanisms to gracefully handle network failures or temporary API outages.
6. **Offline Support and Data Caching**: Develop strategies for providing offline support and data caching in your mobile app, so that users can continue to interact with the app even when they have limited or no network connectivity. This may involve caching data retrieved from your Flask API and synchronizing it when the network connection is restored.
7. **Asynchronous Operations**: For long-running or resource-intensive operations, leverage asynchronous processing techniques in both your Flask API and mobile app. This ensures that the mobile app remains responsive and can continue serving the user while the API handles the heavy lifting in the background.
8. **Versioning and Compatibility**: Align the versioning and evolution of

CHAPTER 8: INTEGRATING FLASK APIS WITH MOBILE FRAMEWORKS

your Flask API with the mobile app development lifecycle. Ensure that your API versioning strategy (as discussed in the previous chapter) is well-documented and communicated to your mobile app development teams, allowing them to plan and execute their integration and migration efforts accordingly.

9. **Monitoring and Feedback Loops**: Implement robust monitoring and logging solutions for both your Flask API and the mobile app integration, allowing you to quickly identify and address any issues or performance bottlenecks. Additionally, establish clear communication channels and feedback mechanisms to gather input from your mobile app users and developers, ensuring a continuous improvement cycle.

By following these best practices, you can build seamless and efficient integrations between your Flask-powered API and the mobile frameworks used in your application development, providing a cohesive and engaging experience for your users.

Offline Support and Data Caching for Mobile Apps

In the mobile app development landscape, providing offline support and data caching is crucial for delivering a responsive and reliable user experience, even in the face of intermittent or poor network connectivity.

When integrating your Flask API with mobile frameworks, you can adopt various strategies to address offline support and data caching requirements:

1. **Caching Responses**: Implement client-side caching mechanisms in your mobile app to store frequently accessed data retrieved from your Flask API. This can be done using built-in caching solutions provided by the mobile development framework, such as the AsyncStorage API in React Native or the Cache class in Flutter.

```
javascript
Copy
```

```javascript
// React Native example
import AsyncStorage from
'@react-native-async-
storage/async-storage';

const fetchUsers = async () => {
  try {
// Check if cached data is available
const cachedUsers = await
 AsyncStorage.getItem('users');
if (cachedUsers) {
return JSON.parse(cachedUsers);
    }

// Fetch data from the API
const response = await
axios.get('/api/users');
await AsyncStorage.setItem('users',
JSON.stringify(response.data));
return response.data;
} catch (error) {
console.error
('Error fetching users:', error);
throw error;
  }
};
```

1. **Offline-first Data Models**: Design your mobile app's data models to work in an offline-first manner, where the app can operate with a local cache of data and synchronize changes with the Flask API when the network connection is restored. This can be achieved using libraries like Realm, SQLite, or Realm.js in React Native, or the sembast package in Flutter.

CHAPTER 8: INTEGRATING FLASK APIS WITH MOBILE FRAMEWORKS

```dart
Copy
// Flutter example using sembast
import 'package:sembast/sembast.dart';

class UserDao {
  final _database = await databaseFactory.openDatabase('users.db');
  final _store = string MapStoreFactory.store('users');

  Future<List<Map<String, dynamic>>> getUsers() async {
    final snapshots = await _store.find(_database);
    return snapshots.map((snapshot) => snapshot.value).toList();
  }

  Future<int> saveUser(User user) async {
    final key = user.id.toString();
    await _store.record(key).put(_database, user.toMap());
    return user.id;
  }
}
```

1. **Conflict Resolution and Synchronization**: Develop a robust conflict resolution and data synchronization strategy to handle situations where the mobile app's local data and the Flask API's data are out of sync. This may involve implementing mechanisms to detect conflicts, prioritize data sources, and ensure data integrity during the synchronization process.

```kotlin
Copy
// Android example using Room and WorkManager
@Dao
interface UserDao {
  @Query("SELECT * FROM users")
  fun getUsers(): List<User>

  @Insert(onConflict =
OnConflictStrategy.REPLACE)
  fun insertUser(user: User)

  @Update
  fun updateUser(user: User)
}

class UserSyncWorker(context:
 Context, params: WorkerParameters)
: CoroutineWorker(context, params) {
  override suspend fun doWork():
 Result {
    try {
val users = userDao.getUsers()
syncWithFlaskApi(users)
return Result.success()
} catch (e: Exception) {
return Result.failure()
    }
  }

  private suspend fun syncWith
FlaskApi(users: List<User>) {
    // Sync users with the Flask API
  }
}
```

1. **Partial Data Syncing and Incremental Updates**: Instead of always fetching and syncing the entire dataset from your Flask API, consider implementing partial data syncing and incremental update mechanisms.

This allows your mobile app to retrieve and update only the necessary data, reducing network traffic and improving the overall user experience.

2. **Background Synchronization**: Leverage the mobile platform's background processing capabilities to periodically sync data between your mobile app and the Flask API, ensuring that users have access to the latest information even when the app is not actively in use. Tools like React Native's BackgroundFetch API or Flutter's FlutterBackgroundService plugin can be used for this purpose.

By incorporating these strategies for offline support and data caching, you can build mobile apps that seamlessly integrate with your Flask-powered API, providing a reliable and responsive user experience, even in the face of intermittent network connectivity.

Conclusion

In this chapter, we've explored the key aspects of integrating your Flask-powered API with popular mobile development frameworks, including React Native, Flutter, and native Android/iOS. We've discussed best practices for API integration, data synchronization, and providing offline support and caching mechanisms to deliver a cohesive and engaging mobile experience for your users.

By aligning your Flask API design and versioning strategy with the needs of mobile app development, you can build robust and scalable integrations that enable your mobile app to leverage the full power of your backend services. Additionally, by implementing strategies for offline support and data caching, you can ensure that your mobile app remains responsive and useful, even in the face of poor or intermittent network connectivity.

As you continue to develop and refine your mobile app and Flask API integration, remember to maintain open communication and collaboration with your mobile app development teams. This will help ensure that the evolving requirements and constraints of both the backend and frontend are effectively addressed, leading to a seamless and user-friendly mobile experience.

Chapter 9: Deploying Flask APIs to Cloud Platforms

As your Flask-powered mobile API backend grows in complexity and usage, the need for reliable and scalable deployment solutions becomes increasingly important. In this chapter, we'll explore various strategies for deploying your Flask API to popular cloud platforms, including containerization, managed services, and serverless architectures.

Containerizing Flask Apps with Docker

One of the most effective ways to package and deploy your Flask API is through the use of Docker containers. Containerization allows you to encapsulate your Flask application, along with its dependencies and runtime environment, into a self-contained and portable package that can be easily deployed to a variety of cloud platforms.

Here's an example of how you can create a Docker image for your Flask API:

```
Dockerfile
Copy
# Use an official Python
runtime as a parent image
FROM python:3.9-slim

# Set the working directory to /app
WORKDIR /app
```

CHAPTER 9: DEPLOYING FLASK APIS TO CLOUD PLATFORMS

```
# Copy the requirements
  file into the container
COPY requirements.txt .

# Install the Python dependencies
RUN pip install --no-cache-dir -r requirements.txt

# Copy the Flask application
code into the container
COPY . .

# Set the environment
  variables for the Flask application
ENV FLASK_APP=app.py
ENV FLASK_ENV=production

# Expose the port that the
  Flask application will run on
EXPOSE 5000

# Start the Flask application
CMD ["flask", "run",
  "--host=0.0.0.0"]
```

In this Dockerfile, we:

1. Use the official Python 3.9 slim image as the base for our container.
2. Set the working directory to /app.
3. Copy the requirements.txt file into the container and install the Python dependencies.
4. Copy the Flask application code into the container.
5. Set the necessary environment variables for the Flask application.
6. Expose port 5000, which is the default port that Flask uses.
7. Define the command to start the Flask application.

Once you have this Dockerfile, you can build the Docker image and push it to a container registry, such as Docker Hub or a private registry provided by your cloud platform.

```bash
Copy
# Build the Docker image
docker build -t my-flask-api .

# Push the image to a registry
docker push my-flask-api:latest
```

With the Docker image available, you can now deploy your Flask API to various cloud platforms that support containerized applications.

Deploying to Managed Services

Cloud platforms often provide managed services that simplify the deployment and management of your Flask API, allowing you to focus on your application rather than the underlying infrastructure.

1. **AWS Elastic Beanstalk**: AWS Elastic Beanstalk is a managed service that automatically handles the deployment, scaling, and monitoring of your Flask API. You can deploy your Docker container or a Flask application directly to Elastic Beanstalk, and it will manage the underlying infrastructure for you.

```bash
Copy
# Create an Elastic Beanstalk application
eb init my-flask-api --platform python

# Create an Elastic Beanstalk environment
eb create my-flask-api-env
```

1. **Google App Engine**: Google App Engine is a managed Platform-as-

CHAPTER 9: DEPLOYING FLASK APIS TO CLOUD PLATFORMS

a-Service (PaaS) that supports the deployment of Flask APIs. You can deploy your Flask application directly to App Engine, and it will automatically handle the scaling, load balancing, and monitoring of your application.

```yaml
yaml
Copy
# app.yaml configuration file
runtime: python39
entrypoint: gunicorn -b :$PORT app:app
```

1. **Azure App Service**: Azure App Service is a managed service from Microsoft that simplifies the deployment and hosting of your Flask API. You can deploy your Flask application directly to App Service, and it will manage the underlying infrastructure and scaling for you.

```
Copy
# Deploy to Azure App Service using the Azure CLI
az webapp up -n my-flask-api
 -g my-resource-group
 --runtime "PYTHON|3.9"
```

In these examples, we're leveraging the managed services provided by AWS, Google, and Microsoft to deploy our Flask API without having to manage the underlying infrastructure. These platforms automatically handle tasks like provisioning compute resources, configuring networking, and setting up monitoring and scaling, allowing you to focus on your application development.

Serverless Deployment with AWS Lambda and Flask-compatible Frameworks

In addition to traditional container-based deployments, you can also leverage serverless architectures to deploy your Flask API. Serverless platforms, such as AWS Lambda, abstract away the underlying infrastructure and allow you to run your Flask API in a fully managed and scalable environment.

To deploy your Flask API to AWS Lambda, you can use a Flask-compatible serverless framework, such as Chalice or Zappa.

1. **Chalice**: Chalice is an open-source Python serverless microframework developed by AWS. It provides a simple and Pythonic way to build and deploy serverless applications, including Flask-powered APIs.

```python
Copy
from chalice import Chalice

app = Chalice(app_name='my-flask-api')

@app.route('/users', methods=['GET'])
def get_users():
    # Your Flask API logic goes here
    return {'users': [{'id': 1, 'name': 'John Doe'}]}
```

1. To deploy your Flask API to AWS Lambda using Chalice, you can run the following commands:

```bash
Copy
# Install the Chalice CLI
pip install chalice

# Create a new Chalice project
chalice new-project my-flask-api

# Deploy the project to AWS Lambda
```

CHAPTER 9: DEPLOYING FLASK APIS TO CLOUD PLATFORMS

```
chalice deploy
```

1. **Zappa**: Zappa is another popular serverless framework that allows you to deploy your Flask API to AWS Lambda. Zappa provides a more direct integration with Flask, making it easier to migrate existing Flask applications to a serverless environment.

```python
Copy
from flask import Flask
import os

app = Flask(__name__)

@app.route('/users', methods=['GET'])
def get_users():
    return {'users':
[{'id': 1, 'name': 'John Doe'}]}

# Zappa configuration
app.config.from_mapping(
    ZAPPA_SETTINGS={
        "dev": {
"app_function": "app.app",
"profile_name": "default",
"project_name": "my-flask-api",
"runtime": "python3.9",
"s3_bucket": "my-zappa-bucket"
        }
    }
)
```

1. To deploy your Flask API to AWS Lambda using Zappa, you can run the following commands:

```bash
Copy
# Install the Zappa CLI
pip install zappa

# Initialize the Zappa configuration
zappa init

# Deploy the project to AWS Lambda
zappa deploy dev
```

Both Chalice and Zappa handle the process of packaging your Flask application, creating the necessary AWS Lambda functions and API Gateway resources, and deploying your API to the serverless environment. This allows you to focus on building your Flask API without worrying about the underlying infrastructure.

Considerations for Choosing a Deployment Strategy

When selecting the appropriate deployment strategy for your Flask API, consider the following factors:

1. **Scalability and Flexibility**: Evaluate the scalability and flexibility requirements of your Flask API. Serverless and managed services like Elastic Beanstalk or App Engine may be more suitable for highly variable and unpredictable traffic patterns, while containerized deployments can provide more control and customization.
2. **Operational Complexity**: Assess your team's expertise and the available resources for managing the operational aspects of your API deployment. Managed services and serverless platforms can significantly reduce the operational complexity, while containerized deployments may require more DevOps expertise.
3. **Cost Optimization**: Analyze the cost implications of each deployment strategy, taking into account factors like compute resources, storage, and data transfer. Serverless and managed services often provide more cost-

CHAPTER 9: DEPLOYING FLASK APIS TO CLOUD PLATFORMS

effective options for applications with variable or intermittent usage patterns.

4. **Integration with Existing Infrastructure**: Consider how the deployment strategy aligns with your organization's existing infrastructure, tooling, and processes. This can help ensure a seamless integration and minimize the overhead of adopting a new deployment approach.
5. **Vendor Lock-in**: Evaluate the level of vendor lock-in associated with each deployment strategy. Containerized deployments may provide more portability, while managed services and serverless platforms may introduce some dependency on the specific cloud provider.
6. **Monitoring and Observability**: Ensure that the chosen deployment strategy supports your requirements for monitoring, logging, and observability, which are crucial for maintaining and troubleshooting your Flask API in production.

By carefully evaluating these factors, you can select the deployment strategy that best suits the needs of your Flask-powered mobile API, balancing operational efficiency, scalability, and cost-effectiveness.

Conclusion

In this chapter, we've explored various strategies for deploying your Flask-powered mobile API to popular cloud platforms, including containerization, managed services, and serverless architectures.

By leveraging Docker containers, you can package your Flask application and its dependencies into a portable and reproducible format, making it easy to deploy to a variety of cloud environments. Additionally, managed services like AWS Elastic Beanstalk, Google App Engine, and Azure App Service provide a streamlined way to deploy and manage your Flask API, abstracting away the underlying infrastructure.

For serverless deployments, frameworks like Chalice and Zappa enable you to run your Flask API on AWS Lambda, taking advantage of the scalability and cost-effectiveness of a fully managed serverless environment.

When choosing the right deployment strategy for your Flask API, consider factors such as scalability, operational complexity, cost optimization, integration with existing infrastructure, and vendor lock-in. By selecting the approach that best aligns with your requirements, you can ensure that your Flask-powered mobile API is deployed and managed in a reliable, scalable, and cost-effective manner.

As you continue to develop and deploy your Flask API, remember to monitor its performance, observe its behavior, and continuously optimize the deployment strategy to meet the evolving needs of your mobile app and its users.

Chapter 10: Extending Flask Capabilities with Extensions

One of the key advantages of using the Flask web framework for building mobile API backends is its modular and extensible nature. Flask, by design, provides a lean and flexible core, and its capabilities can be significantly expanded through the use of various extensions. These extensions allow you to add sophisticated functionality to your Flask API, addressing a wide range of requirements without having to reinvent the wheel.

In this chapter, we'll explore some of the most popular Flask extensions and discuss how you can leverage them to enhance your mobile API solutions.

Leveraging Popular Flask Extensions

1. **Flask-Caching**: Caching is a crucial aspect of building high-performance and scalable APIs, and Flask-Caching is a powerful extension that simplifies the implementation of caching in your Flask applications.

```python
Copy
from flask import Flask
from flask_caching import Cache
```

```python
app = Flask(__name__)
cache = Cache(app, config={
'CACHE_TYPE': 'redis',
'CACHE_REDIS_HOST': 'localhost',
'CACHE_REDIS_PORT': 6379
})

@app.route('/users/<int:user_id>',
 methods=['GET'])
@cache.memoize(timeout=3600)
def get_user(user_id):
# Fetch user data from the database
user = User.query.get(user_id)
return jsonify(user.serialize())
```

1. In this example, we're using the Flask-Caching extension to cache the response of the /users/<int:user_id> endpoint for 1 hour. This can significantly improve the performance of your mobile API by reducing the number of database queries required.
2. **Flask-APScheduler**: Scheduling periodic tasks is a common requirement in mobile API backends, such as generating reports, cleaning up data, or syncing data with external systems. Flask-APScheduler is an extension that integrates the popular APScheduler library with Flask, making it easier to manage scheduled tasks.

```python
Copy
from flask import Flask
from flask_apscheduler import APScheduler

app = Flask(__name__)
scheduler = APScheduler()

def sync_external_data():
```

CHAPTER 10: EXTENDING FLASK CAPABILITIES WITH EXTENSIONS

```
    # Logic to sync data
with an external system
    pass

@scheduler.task('interval',
id='sync_task', seconds=3600, misfire_
grace_time=900)
def scheduled_sync():
    sync_external_data()

if __name__ == '__main__':
    scheduler.init_app(app)
    scheduler.start()
    app.run()
```

1. In this example, we're using the Flask-APScheduler extension to schedule a task that syncs data with an external system every hour.
2. **Flask-SocketIO**: For mobile APIs that require real-time updates and bidirectional communication, such as chat applications or real-time dashboards, the Flask-SocketIO extension provides a seamless integration of the Socket.IO library with Flask.

```python
Copy
from flask import Flask
from flask_socketio import SocketIO, emit

app = Flask(__name__)
socketio = SocketIO(app)

@socketio.on('connect')
def handle_connect():
    print('Client connected')

@socketio.on('disconnect')
```

```
def handle_disconnect():
    print('Client disconnected')

@socketio.on('message')
def handle_message(data):
    print('Received message: ' + data)
    emit('response',
'Server received: ' + data)

if __name__ == '__main__':
    socketio.run(app)
```

1. In this example, we're using the Flask-SocketIO extension to create a WebSocket-based communication channel between the mobile app and the Flask API, enabling real-time updates and bidirectional messaging.
2. **Flask-Restful**: While Flask provides a solid foundation for building APIs, the Flask-Restful extension can further simplify the process of building RESTful APIs by providing a set of abstractions and conventions.

```python
Copy
from flask import Flask
from flask_restful import Resource, Api

app = Flask(__name__)
api = Api(app)

class UserResource(Resource):
    def get(self, user_id):
# Retrieve user data
user = User.query.get(user_id)
return user.serialize()

def post(self):
```

```python
# Create a new user
data = request.get_json()
new_user = User(**data)
db.session.add(new_user)
db.session.commit()
return new_user.serialize(), 201

api.add_resource
(UserResource,
'/users', '/users/<int:user_id>')
```

1. In this example, we're using the Flask-Restful extension to define a UserResource class that handles the /users and /users/<int:user_id> endpoints, simplifying the implementation of the RESTful API logic.
2. **Flask-Migrate**: As your mobile API evolves, managing database schema changes becomes increasingly important. The Flask-Migrate extension, built on top of Alembic, simplifies the process of creating and applying database migrations.

```bash
Copy
# Install Flask-Migrate
pip install flask-migrate

# Initialize the migration repository
flask db init

# Generate a new migration script
flask db migrate -m
"Add user profile picture"

# Apply the migration
flask db upgrade
```

1. With Flask-Migrate, you can easily generate migration scripts based on your data model changes and apply them to your production database, ensuring that your mobile API remains compatible with the underlying data structures.

Selecting and Integrating the Right Extensions for Mobile API Needs

When choosing Flask extensions to enhance your mobile API, it's important to carefully evaluate the specific requirements of your application and select the extensions that best fit your needs. Here are some factors to consider:

1. **Performance and Scalability**: If your mobile API requires high-performance and scalable solutions, extensions like Flask-Caching and Flask-APScheduler can be invaluable for improving the responsiveness and reliability of your API.
2. **Real-time Updates and Bidirectional Communication**: For mobile apps that need to receive real-time updates or engage in bidirectional communication with the backend, the Flask-SocketIO extension can provide a seamless integration of WebSocket-based communication.
3. **RESTful API Design and Conventions**: If you're aiming to build a RESTful API that follows established conventions and best practices, the Flask-Restful extension can simplify the development process and make your API more intuitive for mobile app developers to integrate with.
4. **Database Evolution and Schema Changes**: As your mobile API and its data models evolve over time, the Flask-Migrate extension can help you manage database schema changes and ensure a smooth transition for your mobile app integrations.
5. **Compatibility with Mobile Frameworks**: When selecting extensions, consider how they will integrate with the specific mobile development frameworks you're using (e.g., React Native, Flutter, native Android/iOS). Choose extensions that provide a smooth integration experience and align with the technology stack of your mobile app.
6. **Maintainability and Community Support**: Opt for extensions that

CHAPTER 10: EXTENDING FLASK CAPABILITIES WITH EXTENSIONS

have an active and vibrant community, with regular updates, comprehensive documentation, and a track record of reliable performance. This will ensure the long-term sustainability and supportability of your Flask API.

By carefully evaluating your mobile API requirements and selecting the appropriate Flask extensions, you can significantly enhance the capabilities of your Flask-powered backend, providing a more robust and feature-rich experience for your mobile app users.

Integrating Flask Extensions

Once you've identified the Flask extensions that align with your mobile API requirements, the process of integrating them into your application is generally straightforward. Here's a typical integration workflow:

1. **Install the Extension**: Use pip to install the required Flask extension(s) in your development environment:

```bash
Copy
pip install flask-caching flask-apscheduler flask-socketio flask-restful flask-migrate
```

1. **Configure the Extension**: Configure the extension by following the instructions provided in its documentation. This may involve setting up any necessary configuration parameters, connecting to external services (e.g., caching backends, message queues), or registering the extension with your Flask application.

```python
Copy
from flask import Flask
from flask_caching import Cache

app = Flask(__name__)
app.config.from_object('config')
cache = Cache(app)
```

1. **Integrate the Extension into Your Flask API**: Once the extension is configured, you can start using its features and integrating them into your Flask API implementation. This may involve defining routes, creating resource classes, or leveraging the extension's APIs to add new functionality to your mobile API.

```python
Copy
@app.route('/users/<int:user_id>',
 methods=['GET'])
@cache.memoize(timeout=3600)
def get_user(user_id):
# Fetch user data
from the database and return it
user = User.query.get(user_id)
return jsonify(user.serialize())
```

1. **Test and Validate the Integration**: Thoroughly test the integration of the Flask extension with your mobile API to ensure that it's working as expected. This may involve writing unit tests, integration tests, and end-to-end tests to validate the functionality and performance of your API.
2. **Document the Extension Usage**: Document the usage of the Flask extension within your mobile API's documentation, ensuring that

mobile app developers can easily understand how to leverage the added functionality in their integrations.

By following this integration process, you can seamlessly add powerful capabilities to your Flask-powered mobile API, enhancing the overall functionality and user experience for your mobile app users.

Conclusion

In this chapter, we've explored how you can leverage a wide range of Flask extensions to enhance the capabilities of your mobile API backend. From caching and task scheduling to real-time updates and RESTful API design, the Flask ecosystem provides a rich set of extensions that can help you build more feature-rich and robust mobile API solutions.

By carefully selecting the extensions that best fit the requirements of your mobile app, you can unlock new possibilities for your Flask API, addressing a wide range of needs without having to reinvent the wheel. Whether you're looking to improve performance, implement real-time communication, or simplify the API design process, there's a Flask extension that can help you achieve your goals.

As you continue to develop and enhance your Flask-powered mobile API, remember to stay up-to-date with the latest extensions, their features, and their community support. This will ensure that you can continuously adapt and improve your API to meet the evolving needs of your mobile app and its users.

Part III: Ensuring Robust Flask API Quality Chapter 11: Comprehensive Testing Strategies

In the world of mobile app development, where the backend API is a critical component, ensuring the quality and reliability of your Flask-powered API is paramount. Comprehensive testing strategies play a crucial role in identifying and addressing issues early in the development lifecycle, reducing the risk of production failures and providing a seamless experience for your mobile app users.

In this chapter, we'll explore the various testing approaches you can employ to build a robust and well-tested Flask API, from unit testing individual components to end-to-end testing of the complete mobile app workflow.

Unit Testing Flask API Endpoints and Models

Unit testing is the foundation of a comprehensive testing strategy for your Flask API. By writing unit tests for your API endpoints and data models, you can ensure that each individual component functions as expected, regardless of the state of the overall system.

Here's an example of how you can set up a unit test suite for a Flask API endpoint using the built-in unittest framework:

```
python
Copy
```

```python
import unittest
from flask import json
from app import app, db, User

class TestUserEndpoint
(unittest.TestCase):
def setUp(self):
self.app = app
self.client = self.app.test_client()
self.app_context = self.
app.app_context()
self.app_context.push()
db.create_all()

    def tearDown(self):
db.session.remove()
db.drop_all()
self.app_context.pop()

def test_get_users(self):
# Create some test users
user1 = User(name='John Doe',
 email='john.doe@example.com')
user2 = User(name='Jane Smith',
email='jane.smith@example.com')
db.session.add(user1)
db.session.add(user2)
db.session.commit()

# Make a GET request to the
/users endpoint
response = self.client.get('/users')
self.assertEqual
(response.status_code, 200)

# Verify the response data
data = json.loads(response.data)
self.assertEqual(len(data), 2)
self.assertEqual
(data[0]['name'], 'John Doe')
```

```python
        self.assertEqual
(data[1]['name'], 'Jane Smith')

def test_create_user(self):
    # Make a POST request to the
    /users endpoint
    data = {'name': 'John Doe',
    'email': 'john.doe@example.com'}
    response = self.client.post('/users', data=json.dumps(data),
     content_type='application/json')
    self.assertEqual
(response.status_code, 201)

    # Verify the created user
    user = User.query.filter_by
(email='john.doe@example.com').
first()
    self.assertIsNotNone(user)
    self.assertEqual
(user.name, 'John Doe')

if __name__ == '__main__':
    unittest.main()
```

In this example, we're using the unittest framework to define a test case for the /users endpoint of our Flask API. We're testing the GET and POST methods, ensuring that the endpoint correctly retrieves and creates users in the database.

The setUp() and tearDown() methods are used to set up and tear down the test environment, including creating and dropping the test database tables.

By writing unit tests like these, you can ensure that your Flask API endpoints are functioning correctly, even as you continue to evolve and enhance your application.

Integration Testing with Simulated Mobile App Interactions

While unit testing is essential for verifying the individual components of your Flask API, it's also important to test how these components work together in the context of a mobile app integration. Integration testing allows you to simulate the interactions between your Flask API and the mobile app, ensuring that the two systems work seamlessly as a whole.

Here's an example of how you can set up an integration test using the pytest-flask library:

```python
Copy
import pytest
from flask import json
from app import app, db, User

@pytest.fixture
def client():
    app.config['TESTING'] = True
    with app.test_client() as client:
        with app.app_context():
            db.create_all()
        yield client
        db.session.remove()
        db.drop_all()

def test_get_users(client):
    # Create some test users
    user1 = User(name='John Doe', email='john.doe@example.com')
    user2 = User(name='Jane Smith', email='jane.smith@example.com')
    db.session.add(user1)
    db.session.add(user2)
    db.session.commit()

    # Make a GET request to the
      /users endpoint
    response = client.get('/users')
    assert response.status_code == 200

    # Verify the response data
    data = json.loads(response.data)
    assert len(data) == 2
    assert data[0]['name'] == 'John Doe'
    assert data[1]['name'] == 'Jane Smith'
```

```python
def test_create_user(client):
    # Make a POST request to the
    /users endpoint
    data = {'name': 'John Doe', 'email': 'john.doe@example.com'}
    response = client.post('/users',
     data=json.dumps(data),
     content_type='application/json')
    assert response.status_code == 201

    # Verify the created user
    user = User.query.filter_by
    (email='john.doe@example.com').
    first()
    assert user is not None
    assert user.name == 'John Doe'
```

In this example, we're using the pytest-flask library, which provides a set of fixtures and helpers for testing Flask applications. The client fixture sets up a test client for our Flask app, allowing us to make HTTP requests to our API endpoints.

The test_get_users() and test_create_user() functions simulate interactions with the /users endpoint, creating test users and verifying the responses. This allows us to test the integration between the Flask API and the underlying database, ensuring that the API behaves as expected when interacting with the mobile app.

By writing integration tests like these, you can catch issues that may arise from the interaction between your Flask API and the mobile app, such as data format mismatches, incorrect error handling, or unexpected behavior when dealing with edge cases.

End-to-End Testing for Complete Mobile App Workflows

While unit and integration testing are essential, it's also important to validate the complete end-to-end workflow of your mobile app, including the interaction with the Flask API backend. End-to-end (E2E) testing allows you to simulate the full user journey, from the mobile app's perspective, and ensure that the overall system functions as expected.

For E2E testing of your Flask API and mobile app integration, you can leverage tools like Selenium WebDriver or Appium, which allow you to automate the testing of web-based and mobile applications, respectively.

Here's an example of how you can set up an E2E test using Selenium WebDriver:

```python
Copy
from selenium import webdriver
from selenium.webdriver.
common.by import By
from selenium.webdriver.
support.ui import WebDriverWait
from selenium.webdriver.support import expected_conditions as EC

def test_end_to_end_workflow():
# Start the Selenium WebDriver
driver = webdriver.Chrome()
driver.get('http://localhost:5000')

# Simulate user interactions
 with the mobile app
driver.find_element(
By.ID, 'username').send_keys
('john.doe@example.com')
driver.find_element(By.ID, 'password').send_keys('password')
driver.find_element
(By.ID, 'login').click()

# Wait for the user to be logged in
wait = WebDriverWait(
driver, 10)
dashboard = wait.until(EC.presence_
of_element_located
((By.ID, 'dashboard')))
assert dashboard.is_displayed()

# Interact with the Flask
API through the mobile app
```

```
driver.find_element
(By.ID, 'view-users').click()
user_list = wait.until(EC.presence_
of_element_located
((By.ID, 'user-list')))
assert len(user_list.
find_elements(By.TAG_NAME, 'li')) > 0

    # Clean up
    driver.quit()
```

In this example, we're using Selenium WebDriver to automate the interaction with a web-based mobile app interface. We simulate user actions, such as logging in and viewing the user list, and then verify that the expected UI elements and data are present.

While this example focuses on a web-based mobile app, you can also use Appium to automate the testing of native mobile apps (iOS and Android) and their integration with the Flask API backend.

By implementing comprehensive end-to-end tests, you can ensure that your Flask API and mobile app work seamlessly together, providing a reliable and consistent experience for your users.

Integration with Continuous Integration (CI) and Continuous Deployment (CD)

To ensure that the quality of your Flask API is maintained throughout the development lifecycle, it's essential to integrate your testing strategies with a Continuous Integration (CI) and Continuous Deployment (CD) pipeline.

By incorporating your unit, integration, and end-to-end tests into your CI/CD workflows, you can automatically run the tests on every code change, catch regressions early, and ensure that only high-quality code is deployed to your production environment.

Here's an example of how you can set up a CI/CD pipeline using Travis CI:

```yaml
# .travis.yml
language: python
python:
  - "3.9"

services:
  - postgresql

before_install:
  - pip install -r requirements.txt

script:
  - python -m unittest discover tests/
  - pytest tests/integration/
  - pytest tests/end-to-end/

deploy:
  provider: elasticbeanstalk
  region: "us-west-2"
  app: "my-flask-api"
  env: "my-flask-api-env"
  on:
    branch: main
```

In this example, we're using Travis CI to set up a CI/CD pipeline for our Flask API. The pipeline includes the following steps:

1. Install the required Python dependencies.
2. Run the unit tests using the unittest framework.
3. Run the integration tests using pytest.
4. Run the end-to-end tests using pytest.
5. Deploy the Flask API to AWS Elastic Beanstalk when the tests pass and the code is merged into the main branch.

By integrating your testing strategies with a CI/CD pipeline, you can ensure that the quality of your Flask API is continuously validated and that any regressions or issues are caught early in the development process. This helps maintain the reliability and stability of your mobile API backend, providing a seamless experience for your mobile app users.

Monitoring and Observability

In addition to comprehensive testing, it's also crucial to implement robust monitoring and observability solutions for your Flask API in production. This allows you to quickly identify and address any issues that may arise, ensuring the continued reliability and responsiveness of your mobile API backend.

Some key monitoring and observability techniques include:

1. **Logging and Error Tracking**: Implement comprehensive logging mechanisms in your Flask API, capturing both application-level and system-level events. Use tools like Sentry or Datadog to centralize and analyze your logs, enabling you to quickly identify and resolve errors or performance issues.
2. **Metrics and Performance Monitoring**: Collect and monitor key metrics, such as request latency, error rates, and resource utilization, to gain insights into the performance and health of your Flask API. Tools like Prometheus, Grafana, or AWS CloudWatch can be used to visualize and analyze these metrics.
3. **Distributed Tracing**: For complex mobile API backends that involve multiple services or external dependencies, implement distributed tracing solutions like Jaeger or AWS X-Ray. These tools allow you to trace the flow of requests through your system, identify performance bottlenecks, and quickly debug issues.
4. **Synthetic Monitoring**: Set up synthetic monitoring, where you simulate user interactions with your mobile app and Flask API, to proactively detect and address issues before they impact your real users. Tools like Pingdom or New Relic can be used for this purpose.
5. **Alerting and Incident Management**: Configure alerting mechanisms to notify your team of critical events or performance degradation, enabling a rapid response to issues. Integrate your monitoring tools

with incident management platforms like PagerDuty or Opsgenie to streamline the incident response process.

By implementing a comprehensive monitoring and observability strategy, you can ensure the continued reliability and responsiveness of your Flask-powered mobile API, quickly identifying and resolving any issues that may arise in production.

Conclusion

In this chapter, we've explored the importance of comprehensive testing strategies for building robust and reliable Flask-powered mobile API backends. From unit testing individual components to integration testing with simulated mobile app interactions and end-to-end testing of the complete workflow, we've covered a range of techniques to ensure the quality and reliability of your Flask API.

By integrating your testing strategies with a Continuous Integration and Continuous Deployment pipeline, you can automate the validation of your Flask API, catch regressions early, and ensure that only high-quality code is deployed to production.

Additionally, we've discussed the importance of monitoring and observability, which allow you to quickly identify and address issues in your production environment, maintaining the reliability and responsiveness of your mobile API backend.

As you continue to develop and maintain your Flask-powered mobile API, remember to continuously review and refine your testing and monitoring strategies, adapting them to the evolving requirements of your mobile app and the changing landscape of the Flask ecosystem. By prioritizing quality and reliability, you can build mobile API backends that provide a seamless and delightful experience for your users.

Chapter 12: Securing Flask APIs

In the modern digital landscape, the security of your Flask-powered mobile API is of paramount importance. As the backend that powers your mobile application, your API handles sensitive user data and provides access to critical functionality. Ensuring the security of your Flask API is essential to building trust with your users and protecting your application from malicious attacks.

In this chapter, we'll explore best practices for securing your Flask API, covering topics such as authentication and authorization, protecting sensitive data, and implementing measures to safeguard against common API vulnerabilities and attacks.

Authentication and Authorization Best Practices

Implementing robust authentication and authorization mechanisms is a crucial aspect of securing your Flask API. This ensures that only authorized users and clients can access the appropriate data and functionality within your API.

1. **Token-based Authentication**: As discussed in the previous chapters, token-based authentication, such as the use of JSON Web Tokens (JWT), is a widely adopted approach for securing mobile API backends. This approach provides several benefits, including stateless authentication, reduced server-side complexity, and improved scalability. When implementing token-based authentication in your Flask API, follow these best practices:

CHAPTER 12: SECURING FLASK APIS

- Use a secure and long-lasting secret key for signing the JWT tokens.
- Ensure that the token expiration time is set to a reasonable duration based on your application's security requirements.
- Implement token revocation mechanisms to invalidate tokens when necessary (e.g., upon user logout).
- Validate the token's integrity, expiration, and other claims before granting access to API resources.

1. **Role-based Access Control (RBAC)**: In addition to user authentication, it's important to implement fine-grained access control mechanisms to ensure that users can only perform actions and access data that they're authorized to. One common approach is to use Role-based Access Control (RBAC), where each user is assigned a specific role, and each role is granted a set of permissions. When implementing RBAC in your Flask API, consider the following best practices:

- Define a clear and comprehensive set of roles and permissions that align with your application's requirements.
- Maintain a centralized source of truth for role and permission definitions, and ensure that it's easily accessible and maintainable.
- Implement a flexible and extensible RBAC system that can adapt to changing business requirements and security needs.
- Regularly review and audit the assigned roles and permissions to ensure that they remain relevant and appropriate.

1. **Multi-factor Authentication**: For added security, consider implementing multi-factor authentication (MFA) for your Flask API. This involves requiring users to provide additional forms of authentication, such as a one-time code sent to their mobile device, in addition to their username and password. While MFA may add some complexity to the user experience, it significantly enhances the security of your API by making it more difficult for attackers to gain unauthorized access, even if they obtain a user's credentials.

2. **Secure Password Handling**: When handling user passwords in your Flask API, it's crucial to follow best practices for secure password storage and management. This includes:

- Hashing passwords using a secure algorithm (e.g., Bcrypt, Argon2) with appropriate salt values.
- Avoiding storing plaintext passwords or using weak hashing algorithms (e.g., MD5, SHA-1).
- Enforcing strong password policies, such as minimum length, complexity requirements, and password expiration.
- Providing secure password reset mechanisms that don't expose the actual password.

By following these best practices for authentication and authorization, you can ensure that your Flask API is properly secured and that only authorized users and clients can access the sensitive data and functionality within your application.

Protecting Sensitive Data and Preventing Common API Vulnerabilities

In addition to implementing robust authentication and authorization mechanisms, it's essential to protect the sensitive data handled by your Flask API and address common API vulnerabilities.

1. **Sensitive Data Handling**: Ensure that all sensitive data, such as user information, financial data, or confidential business details, is properly secured and protected within your Flask API. This includes:

- Encrypting sensitive data at rest (e.g., using database encryption or file-level encryption).
- Encrypting sensitive data in transit (e.g., using HTTPS/SSL/TLS).
- Implementing access controls and logging mechanisms to monitor and audit access to sensitive data.
- Regularly reviewing and updating your data protection policies and practices to stay current with industry standards and regulations.

1. **Input Validation and Sanitization**: Implement comprehensive input validation and sanitization mechanisms in your Flask API to protect against common vulnerabilities, such as SQL injection, cross-site scripting (XSS), and command injection.

- Validate all user input, including query parameters, request bodies, and headers, to ensure that they conform to expected formats and data types.
- Use Flask's built-in request.get_json() method or a library like flask-restful to automatically validate and parse incoming JSON data.
- Sanitize and escape all user input before using it in database queries, template rendering, or other sensitive operations.

1. **API Versioning and Deprecation**: As discussed in the previous chapter, it's important to have a well-defined strategy for versioning and deprecating your Flask API. This not only helps maintain compatibility with your mobile app integrations but also enhances the overall security of your API.

- Clearly communicate the versioning scheme and deprecation timeline to your mobile app developers.
- Maintain backwards compatibility as much as possible to minimize the impact of API changes on your mobile app integrations.
- Promptly deprecate and remove old API versions to reduce the attack surface and the risk of exploiting vulnerabilities in legacy versions.

1. **API Endpoint and Parameter Naming**: Choose descriptive but non-revealing names for your Flask API endpoints and parameters. Avoid using names that could expose sensitive information or provide clues about your application's internal structure.

- Use generic names for API endpoints (e.g., /users instead of /employee_details).
- Avoid including sensitive information (e.g., user IDs, account numbers)

in URL paths or query parameters.
- Use appropriate HTTP status codes and error messages that don't leak sensitive details.

1. **Rate Limiting and DoS Protection**: Implement rate limiting and protection against Denial-of-Service (DoS) attacks to safeguard your Flask API from abuse and ensure the availability of your services.

- Use a rate-limiting solution, such as the flask-limiter extension, to restrict the number of requests a client can make within a given time frame.
- Configure appropriate rate limits for different types of API endpoints (e.g., read-only vs. write operations).
- Implement techniques to mitigate the impact of DoS attacks, such as request queueing, IP-based blocking, or client authentication requirements.

By following these best practices for protecting sensitive data and addressing common API vulnerabilities, you can significantly enhance the overall security posture of your Flask-powered mobile API.

Implementing Rate Limiting and DoS Protection

Rate limiting and protection against Denial-of-Service (DoS) attacks are crucial components of a comprehensive security strategy for your Flask API. These measures help safeguard your API from abuse, ensure the availability of your services, and mitigate the impact of malicious attempts to overwhelm your system.

1. **Rate Limiting with Flask-Limiter**: The Flask-Limiter extension provides a simple and effective way to implement rate limiting in your Flask API. Here's an example of how you can use it:

CHAPTER 12: SECURING FLASK APIS

```python
Copy
from flask import Flask
from flask_limiter import Limiter
from flask_limiter.util
  import get_remote_address

app = Flask(__name__)
limiter = Limiter(
    app,
key_func=get_remote_address,
default_limits=
["200 per day", "50 per hour"]
)

@app.route('/users', methods=['GET'])
@limiter.limit("10 per minute")
def get_users():
# Fetch and return user data
return jsonify(users)
```

1. In this example, we're using the Flask-Limiter extension to:

- Limit the number of requests to the /users endpoint to 10 per minute.
- Limit the overall number of requests to 200 per day and 50 per hour, based on the client's IP address.

1. You can customize the rate limiting rules based on your API's specific requirements and the expected usage patterns.
2. **DoS Protection with Nginx and iptables**: To protect your Flask API from Denial-of-Service (DoS) attacks, you can implement a multi-layered defense strategy using Nginx and iptables:

- **Nginx Configuration**:
- Configure Nginx to act as a reverse proxy in front of your Flask API.
- Enable Nginx's built-in DoS protection features, such as limiting the

number of connections per client IP address and setting appropriate timeouts.
- Use Nginx's request queue to buffer incoming requests and prevent your Flask API from being overwhelmed.
- **iptables Configuration**:
- Use iptables, the Linux firewall, to implement additional IP-based blocking and rate limiting rules.
- Configure iptables to automatically block IP addresses that exceed a certain number of requests within a given time frame.
- Implement safeguards to prevent IP address spoofing and other common DoS attack techniques.

1. By combining the rate limiting capabilities of Flask-Limiter with the DoS protection features of Nginx and iptables, you can create a robust and multi-layered defense system to safeguard your Flask API from abuse and ensure its availability.
2. **Monitoring and Alerting**: Complementing your rate limiting and DoS protection measures, it's essential to implement comprehensive monitoring and alerting mechanisms to detect and respond to potential security incidents.

- **Monitoring**:
- Monitor your Flask API's performance metrics, such as request rates, response times, and error rates.
- Analyze the logs to identify unusual activity patterns that may indicate an ongoing attack.
- Use tools like Prometheus, Grafana, or AWS CloudWatch to visualize and analyze your API's security-related metrics.
- **Alerting**:
- Configure alerting rules to notify your security team of anomalous events, such as sudden spikes in request rates or unusual error patterns.
- Integrate your monitoring solution with incident management platforms like PagerDuty or Opsgenie to streamline the incident response process.

- Establish clear incident response procedures and communication channels to effectively address and mitigate security incidents.

By implementing a comprehensive security strategy that includes rate limiting, DoS protection, and robust monitoring and alerting, you can significantly enhance the overall security posture of your Flask-powered mobile API, ensuring the availability and reliability of your services for your mobile app users.

Conclusion

In this chapter, we've explored the essential aspects of securing your Flask-powered mobile API, focusing on best practices for authentication and authorization, protecting sensitive data, and implementing measures to safeguard against common API vulnerabilities and attacks.

By leveraging token-based authentication, implementing role-based access control (RBAC), and considering multi-factor authentication, you can ensure that only authorized users and clients can access the appropriate data and functionality within your API.

Additionally, we've discussed the importance of properly handling sensitive data, validating and sanitizing user input, and maintaining a well-defined API versioning and deprecation strategy to enhance the overall security of your Flask API.

To protect your API from abuse and ensure its availability, we've covered the implementation of rate limiting and Denial-of-Service (DoS) protection using tools like Flask-Limiter, Nginx, and iptables, along with the importance of comprehensive monitoring and alerting mechanisms.

By incorporating these security best practices into the development and deployment of your Flask-powered mobile API, you can build a robust and trustworthy backend that safeguards your users' data and provides a secure foundation for your mobile application.

As you continue to enhance the security of your Flask API, remember to stay up-to-date with the latest security threats, industry standards, and regulatory requirements. Regularly review and update your security policies and practices to ensure that your API remains resilient and adaptable in the face of evolving security challenges.

Chapter 13: Monitoring and Troubleshooting Flask APIs

In the world of mobile app development, where the backend API is a critical component, ensuring the reliability and responsiveness of your Flask-powered API is of utmost importance. Effective monitoring and troubleshooting strategies play a crucial role in identifying and addressing issues before they impact your mobile app users.

In this chapter, we'll explore the various techniques and tools you can leverage to monitor the performance and health of your Flask API, as well as common problems that may arise and how to efficiently troubleshoot and resolve them.

Logging and Error Handling for Mobile API Issues

Comprehensive logging and effective error handling are the foundation of a robust monitoring and troubleshooting strategy for your Flask API. By capturing and analyzing relevant logs, you can quickly identify the root causes of issues and take appropriate actions to resolve them.

1. **Logging in Flask**: Flask provides a built-in logging mechanism that you can leverage to record various events and information about your API. You can configure the logging level, format, and output destination to suit your needs.

```python
Copy
import logging
from flask import Flask

app = Flask(__name__)

# Configure logging
logging.basicConfig(
level=logging.INFO,
format='%(asctime)s
 %(levelname)s: %(message)s',
datetimeFormat=
'%Y-%m-%d %H:%M:%S',
filename='api.log'
)

@app.route('/users/<int:user_id>', methods=['GET'])
def get_user(user_id):
    try:
# Retrieve user data
user = User.query.get(user_id)
if user is None:
logging.warning
(f'User with ID {user_id} not found')
return jsonify
({'error': 'User not found'}), 404
return jsonify
(user.serialize())
except Exception as e:
logging.error
(f'Error retrieving user:
 {str(e)}')
return jsonify
({'error':
 'Internal server error'}), 500
```

1. In this example, we've configured the logging system to record messages

CHAPTER 13: MONITORING AND TROUBLESHOOTING FLASK APIS

at the INFO level or higher, with a custom format and output to a file named api.log. Within the get_user() function, we're logging warning messages when a user is not found and error messages when an exception occurs.

2. **Structured Logging and Log Aggregation**: While the built-in Flask logging is a good starting point, you may want to consider using a more structured logging approach and aggregating your logs for better analysis and troubleshooting. Tools like Sentry, Datadog, or Logstash can help you achieve this. These tools allow you to capture structured log data, including contextual information, and centralize the logging from your Flask API and other components of your mobile app ecosystem. This makes it easier to search, analyze, and correlate logs, helping you quickly identify and resolve issues.

3. **Error Handling and Reporting**: Implement a comprehensive error handling strategy in your Flask API to provide clear and informative error messages to your mobile app users, while also capturing detailed information for troubleshooting purposes.

```python
Copy
from flask import Flask, jsonify
from werkzeug.exceptions
import HTTPException

app = Flask(__name__)

@app.errorhandler(Exception)
def handle_exception(e):
if isinstance(e, HTTPException):
return jsonify
({'error': e.description}), e.code
    else:
logging.error
(f'Unhandled exception: {str(e)}')
```

FLASK API FOR MOBILE APP DEVELOPMENT

```
return jsonify
({'error': 'Internal
server error'}), 500

@app.route('/users/
<int:user_id>',
 methods=['GET'])
def get_user(user_id):
    try:
# Retrieve user data
user = User.query.get(user_id)
if user is None:
raise Exception
(f'User with ID
{user_id} not found')
return jsonify(user.serialize())
except Exception as e:
raise e
```

1. In this example, we've implemented a global error handler that captures both HTTP exceptions (e.g., 404 Not Found) and unhandled exceptions. For HTTP exceptions, we return a JSON response with the appropriate error message and status code. For unhandled exceptions, we log the error and return a generic "Internal server error" message to the mobile app.

By implementing comprehensive logging and effective error handling, you can create a robust foundation for monitoring and troubleshooting your Flask-powered mobile API, making it easier to identify and address issues that may arise.

Monitoring API Performance and Detecting Anomalies

Monitoring the performance and health of your Flask API is essential for ensuring a seamless user experience for your mobile app users. By tracking key metrics and detecting anomalies, you can proactively identify and address issues before they impact your application.

CHAPTER 13: MONITORING AND TROUBLESHOOTING FLASK APIS

1. **Metrics and Performance Monitoring**: Collect and monitor a range of metrics to gain insights into the performance and overall health of your Flask API. Some key metrics to consider include:

- Request latency: Track the response times for your API endpoints.
- Error rates: Monitor the frequency and types of errors occurring in your API.
- Resource utilization: Monitor the CPU, memory, and network usage of your API backend.
- Throughput: Track the number of requests your API can handle over time.

1. Tools like Prometheus, Grafana, or AWS CloudWatch can help you collect, visualize, and analyze these metrics, allowing you to identify performance bottlenecks and trends.
2. **Distributed Tracing**: For complex mobile API backends that involve multiple services or external dependencies, implement distributed tracing solutions like Jaeger or AWS X-Ray. These tools allow you to trace the flow of requests through your system, identify performance issues, and quickly debug problems. By leveraging distributed tracing, you can gain visibility into the end-to-end execution of your API requests, including the time spent in each component and the dependencies between them. This can be particularly useful for troubleshooting issues related to slow response times, data inconsistencies, or failures in external integrations.
3. **Synthetic Monitoring**: Set up synthetic monitoring, where you simulate user interactions with your mobile app and Flask API, to proactively detect and address issues before they impact your real users. Tools like Pingdom, New Relic, or Uptime.com can be used for this purpose. Synthetic monitoring allows you to regularly test your API endpoints, simulate common user flows, and verify the expected behavior and performance, even when there is no real user traffic. This can help you identify issues such as broken endpoints, slow response times, or unexpected error conditions.

4. **Anomaly Detection**: Implement anomaly detection mechanisms to identify unusual patterns or deviations in your API's performance and usage metrics. This can help you quickly detect and respond to potential security incidents, such as DDoS attacks, API abuse, or unexpected spikes in traffic. Tools like AWS CloudWatch, Datadog, or Prometheus provide built-in anomaly detection capabilities that can be configured to trigger alerts when your API's behavior deviates from the expected norm.

By implementing a comprehensive monitoring strategy that includes performance metrics, distributed tracing, synthetic monitoring, and anomaly detection, you can gain deep visibility into the health and performance of your Flask-powered mobile API, enabling you to proactively identify and address issues before they impact your mobile app users.

Common Problems and Solutions for Flask-Powered Mobile Backends

As you develop and maintain your Flask-powered mobile API, you may encounter various challenges and issues. Here are some common problems and suggested solutions to help you troubleshoot and resolve them effectively.

1. **Slow API Response Times**:

- **Causes**: Database queries taking too long, inefficient code, resource-intensive operations, or high concurrency.
- **Solutions**: Optimize database queries, implement caching strategies, offload long-running tasks to background workers, and scale your infrastructure (e.g., add more app instances, use a more powerful database).

1. **High Error Rates**:

- **Causes**: Incorrect or missing input validation, unhandled exceptions, issues in external integrations, or errors in the mobile app integration.
- **Solutions**: Enhance input validation, implement comprehensive error

CHAPTER 13: MONITORING AND TROUBLESHOOTING FLASK APIS

handling, monitor external service dependencies, and improve communication with the mobile app development team.

1. **Unexpected Behavior or Inconsistent Data:**

- **Causes**: Race conditions, data synchronization issues, or problems with database transactions.
- **Solutions**: Implement proper locking mechanisms, use database transactions, and ensure data consistency across your API and the mobile app.

1. **Security Vulnerabilities:**

- **Causes**: Weak authentication and authorization, unprotected sensitive data, or common API vulnerabilities (e.g., SQL injection, cross-site scripting).
- **Solutions**: Follow best practices for authentication, authorization, and data protection, and address common API security issues.

1. **Sudden Spikes in Traffic or API Abuse:**

- **Causes**: Unexpected user behavior, bot activity, or Denial-of-Service (DoS) attacks.
- **Solutions**: Implement rate limiting, IP-based blocking, and other DoS protection measures, and monitor for anomalous traffic patterns.

1. **Difficulty Upgrading or Migrating API Versions:**

- **Causes**: Lack of a clear versioning strategy, insufficient documentation, or breaking changes in the API.
- **Solutions**: Establish a versioning convention, provide comprehensive migration guides, maintain backwards compatibility, and communicate changes to mobile app developers.

1. **Integrating with Mobile Frameworks**:

   - **Causes**: Incompatible data formats, authentication issues, or problems with offline support and data synchronization.
   - **Solutions**: Ensure consistent data formats, implement secure authentication mechanisms, and develop robust strategies for offline support and data caching.

When troubleshooting issues in your Flask-powered mobile API, follow these general steps:

1. **Gather Relevant Information**: Collect relevant logs, metrics, and traces to understand the scope and nature of the problem.
2. **Isolate the Issue**: Identify the specific component(s) or integration points that are causing the problem.
3. **Analyze the Root Cause**: Examine the gathered information to determine the underlying cause of the issue.
4. **Implement a Solution**: Based on the root cause analysis, develop and implement a solution to address the problem.
5. **Validate the Fix**: Test the solution to ensure that the issue has been resolved and that no new problems have been introduced.
6. **Document and Share Learnings**: Document the issue, the solution, and any key learnings, and share them with your team to prevent similar problems in the future.

By following these troubleshooting steps and addressing the common problems discussed in this chapter, you can effectively maintain the reliability and responsiveness of your Flask-powered mobile API, ensuring a seamless experience for your mobile app users.

Conclusion

In this chapter, we've explored the essential aspects of monitoring and troubleshooting your Flask-powered mobile API, which are crucial for ensuring the reliability and responsiveness of your backend services.

CHAPTER 13: MONITORING AND TROUBLESHOOTING FLASK APIS

We've discussed the importance of comprehensive logging and effective error handling, which provide the foundation for identifying and addressing issues that may arise in your Flask API. By leveraging structured logging and log aggregation tools, you can gain better visibility into the behavior and performance of your API, making it easier to detect and resolve problems.

Additionally, we've covered various monitoring techniques, such as performance metrics, distributed tracing, synthetic monitoring, and anomaly detection, that can help you proactively identify and address issues before they impact your mobile app users. These monitoring strategies enable you to gain deep insights into the health and performance of your Flask API, allowing you to make informed decisions and take appropriate actions.

Finally, we've explored common problems and solutions that you may encounter when maintaining a Flask-powered mobile API backend, covering a range of issues related to performance, security, versioning, and mobile app integration. By understanding these common challenges and following the recommended troubleshooting steps, you can efficiently address and resolve issues, ensuring the continued reliability and responsiveness of your Flask API.

As you continue to develop and maintain your Flask-powered mobile API, remember to continuously review and refine your monitoring and troubleshooting strategies, adapting them to the evolving requirements of your mobile app and the changing landscape of the Flask ecosystem. By prioritizing observability and responsiveness, you can build mobile API backends that provide a seamless and delightful experience for your users.

Chapter 14: Best Practices and Coding Exercises

In the journey of building a production-ready Flask API for mobile applications, it's essential to not only implement the core functionality but also adhere to best practices, apply sound design principles, and optimize the API's performance and scalability. This chapter will focus on providing hands-on coding exercises, design pattern discussions, and optimization techniques to help you solidify your understanding and skills in developing robust and efficient Flask APIs for mobile app backends.

Hands-on Coding Challenges and Project-based Tutorials

Engaging in practical coding exercises and project-based tutorials is a powerful way to reinforce the concepts and techniques you've learned throughout this book. By working through real-world scenarios and implementing solutions, you'll deepen your understanding of Flask and gain valuable experience in building production-ready mobile API backends.

1. **User Management API**: Create a Flask API that handles user management functionalities, such as registration, authentication, user profile updates, and password resets. Implement features like token-based authentication, role-based access control, and password hashing for secure user management.

CHAPTER 14: BEST PRACTICES AND CODING EXERCISES

```python
Copy
from flask import Flask,
 jsonify, request
from flask_jwt_extended
import JWTManager,
jwt_required, create_access_token
from werkzeug.security import
 generate_password_hash,
 check_password_hash
from flask_sqlalchemy import SQLAlchemy

app = Flask(__name__)
app.config['JWT_SECRET_KEY']
= 'your-secret-key'
jwt = JWTManager(app)
db = SQLAlchemy(app)

class User(db.Model):
id = db.Column
(db.Integer, primary_key=True)
username = db.Column
(db.String(50), unique=True,
 nullable=False)
email = db.Column
(db.String(120),
unique=True, nullable=False)
password_hash =
db.Column(db.String(100),
nullable=False)
role = db.Column
(db.String(20), default='user')

def set_password(self, password):
self.password_hash =
generate_password_
hash(password)

def check_password
(self, password):
```

```
return check_password_
hash(self.password_hash
, password)

# Implement user 
registration, authentication,
 and other features
```

1. **Geolocation-based API**: Build a Flask API that retrieves and processes geolocation data, such as nearby points of interest, weather information, or traffic updates. Integrate with relevant third-party APIs and use techniques like caching and asynchronous processing to optimize the API's performance.

```python
Copy
from flask import Flask, jsonify
from flask_caching import Cache
from celery import Celery
import requests

app = Flask(__name__)
cache = Cache(app, config={'CACHE_TYPE': 'redis'})
celery = Celery(app.name, broker='redis://localhost:6379/0')

@app.route('/weather/<
latitude>/<longitude>
', methods=['GET'])
@cache.memoize(timeout=3600)
def get_weather
(latitude, longitude):
    return fetch_
weather_data.delay
(latitude, longitude).get()
```

CHAPTER 14: BEST PRACTICES AND CODING EXERCISES

```
@celery.task
def fetch_weather_
data(latitude, longitude):
weather_api_url =
 f'https://api.openweathermap.
org/data/2.5/weather?
lat={latitude}&lon=
{longitude}&appid=YOUR_API_KEY'
response = requests.
get(weather_api_url)
return response.json()
```

1. **Payments API**: Develop a Flask API that handles secure payment processing, including features like creating payment intents, handling webhook notifications, and managing customer information. Leverage third-party payment gateways and implement best practices for PCI compliance.

```python
Copy
from flask import Flask, jsonify, request
import stripe

app = Flask(__name__)
app.config['STRIPE_SECRET_KEY'] = 'your_stripe_secret_key'
stripe.api_key = app.config['STRIPE_SECRET_KEY']

@app.route('/create_payment_intent', methods=['POST'])
def create_payment_intent():
    data = request.get_json()
    amount = data['amount']
    payment_intent = stripe.PaymentIntent.create(
```

```python
        amount=amount,
        currency='usd',
        payment_method_types=['card']
    )
    return jsonify
({'client_secret':
payment_intent.client_secret})

@app.route('/webhook',
 methods=['POST'])
def handle_webhook():
    event = None
    try:
event = stripe.Event.
construct_from(
request.get_data(),
 stripe.api_key
        )
    except ValueError as e:
    return jsonify
({'error': str(e)}), 400

    # Handle the event
    if event.type ==
'payment_intent.succeeded':
payment_intent = event.data.object
        # Fulfill any orders
or mark the payment as successful
    return jsonify({'success': True})
```

These coding exercises and project-based tutorials will help you apply the knowledge you've gained throughout the book, solidifying your understanding of Flask API development and preparing you to tackle more complex real-world scenarios.

Applying Design Patterns and Architectural Principles

In addition to hands-on coding exercises, it's essential to understand and apply sound design patterns and architectural principles when building production-ready Flask APIs for mobile applications. This will ensure that

CHAPTER 14: BEST PRACTICES AND CODING EXERCISES

your API is scalable, maintainable, and adaptable to changing requirements.

1. **Separation of Concerns**: Implement a clear separation of concerns in your Flask API, dividing the codebase into distinct layers (e.g., routes, services, data access) to promote modularity, testability, and easier long-term maintenance.
2. **Repository Pattern**: Utilize the Repository pattern to encapsulate the data access logic, abstracting the underlying database implementation and providing a consistent interface for your API services.
3. **Service Layer**: Introduce a service layer that handles the core business logic of your API, separating it from the routing and presentation concerns. This promotes reusability, testability, and separation of concerns.
4. **Dependency Injection**: Apply the Dependency Injection principle to decouple your API components and promote testability. Use a dependency injection framework like Flask-Injector or Dependency Injector to manage the creation and injection of dependencies.
5. **Event-driven Architecture**: Implement an event-driven architecture in your Flask API, using a message queue or event bus to decouple the processing of long-running or asynchronous tasks from the main request-response flow.
6. **Circuit Breaker Pattern**: Incorporate the Circuit Breaker pattern to protect your Flask API from cascading failures when integrating with external services or components. This helps maintain the overall availability and resilience of your API.
7. **Versioning and Backward Compatibility**: Adhere to the principles of versioning and backward compatibility, as discussed in the previous chapters, to ensure a smooth evolution of your Flask API and minimize the impact on your mobile app integrations.

By understanding and applying these design patterns and architectural principles, you can build Flask APIs that are scalable, maintainable, and adaptable to the evolving needs of your mobile application.

Optimization Techniques for Mobile-focused Flask APIs

As you develop and deploy your Flask API to power your mobile application, it's crucial to consider optimization techniques that will enhance the performance, scalability, and efficiency of your API. Here are some key optimization strategies to keep in mind:

1. **Database Optimization**:

- Implement efficient database queries and indexing strategies to minimize the load on your database.
- Consider using a more scalable database solution, such as a distributed or NoSQL database, if your API requires handling large data volumes or high concurrency.
- Leverage database caching mechanisms, such as Redis or Memcached, to offload frequently accessed data from the primary database.

1. **Caching and Content Delivery Network (CDN)**:

- Use caching techniques, like the ones demonstrated with the Flask-Caching extension, to store and serve frequently accessed data, reducing the load on your API.
- Integrate a Content Delivery Network (CDN) to handle the delivery of static assets, such as images or CSS/JS files, improving the overall responsiveness of your mobile app.

1. **Asynchronous Processing**:

- Offload long-running or resource-intensive tasks to background workers using tools like Celery or RQ, ensuring that your Flask API can continue serving other requests without delay.
- Implement asynchronous programming techniques in your Flask API to handle I/O-bound operations, such as network requests or file operations, more efficiently.

CHAPTER 14: BEST PRACTICES AND CODING EXERCISES

1. **Scalability and Load Balancing**:

- Design your Flask API with horizontal scalability in mind, allowing you to easily add more instances to handle increasing traffic loads.
- Implement load balancing mechanisms, such as using a reverse proxy like Nginx or a cloud-based load balancer, to distribute the incoming requests across multiple Flask API instances.
- Leverage container orchestration platforms like Docker Swarm or Kubernetes to automate the scaling and deployment of your Flask API.

1. **Monitoring and Observability**:

- Integrate comprehensive monitoring and observability solutions, as discussed in the previous chapter, to gain visibility into the performance and health of your Flask API.
- Use the collected metrics and data to identify performance bottlenecks and optimize your API accordingly.

1. **API Documentation and Developer Experience**:

- Provide clear and comprehensive API documentation, using tools like Swagger/OpenAPI or Postman, to improve the developer experience and facilitate easier integration with your mobile app.
- Implement features like API versioning, error handling, and client libraries to enhance the usability and maintainability of your Flask API for mobile app developers.

By applying these optimization techniques, you can ensure that your Flask API is scalable, performant, and well-suited to power the backend of your mobile application, delivering a seamless and responsive experience for your users.

Coding Exercises and Project Walkthroughs

To further reinforce the concepts and techniques covered in this chapter, let's go through a few coding exercises and project-based walkthroughs:

1. **Coding Exercise: Implementing the Repository Pattern**: Refactor the user management API example from the earlier coding challenge to use the Repository pattern. Create a separate UserRepository class that encapsulates the data access logic, and update the service layer to use this repository.
2. **Project Walkthrough: Building a Geolocation-based API with Caching and Asynchronous Processing**: Follow the steps outlined in the geolocation-based API example to build a Flask API that retrieves and processes location-based data. Implement caching using Flask-Caching and offload the data fetching to background workers using Celery.
3. **Coding Exercise: Applying the Circuit Breaker Pattern**: Extend the payments API example to incorporate the Circuit Breaker pattern when integrating with the Stripe payment gateway. Use a library like Flask-CircuitBreaker to manage the circuit breaker logic and ensure the resilience of your API.
4. **Project Walkthrough: Optimizing a Flask API for Mobile Deployment**: Take an existing Flask API project and apply the optimization techniques discussed in this chapter. This may include database optimization, caching strategies, asynchronous processing, and load balancing. Deploy the optimized API to a cloud platform and measure the performance improvements.

By working through these coding exercises and project walkthroughs, you'll have the opportunity to deeply engage with the best practices, design patterns, and optimization techniques covered in this chapter, solidifying your skills in building robust and efficient Flask APIs for mobile app backends.

Conclusion

In this final chapter of the "Building Production-Ready Flask APIs" section, we've explored the importance of best practices, coding exercises, and optimization techniques for ensuring the quality and robustness of your Flask-powered mobile API.

CHAPTER 14: BEST PRACTICES AND CODING EXERCISES

Through hands-on coding challenges and project-based tutorials, you've had the chance to apply the knowledge and skills you've gained throughout the book, reinforcing your understanding of Flask API development and preparing you to tackle more complex real-world scenarios.

We've also discussed the application of design patterns and architectural principles, such as Separation of Concerns, Repository Pattern, and Event-driven Architecture, which can help you build scalable, maintainable, and adaptable Flask APIs that align with industry best practices.

Finally, we've delved into various optimization techniques, including database optimization, caching and CDN integration, asynchronous processing, and scalability strategies, to ensure that your Flask API can effectively power the backend of your mobile application, delivering a seamless and responsive experience for your users.

By incorporating the best practices, coding exercises, and optimization strategies covered in this chapter, you'll be well-equipped to develop and deploy production-ready Flask APIs that not only meet the functional requirements of your mobile app but also demonstrate the qualities of robustness, scalability, and efficiency that are essential for success in the mobile app ecosystem.

As you continue your journey of building and maintaining Flask-powered mobile API backends, remember to stay curious, keep learning, and constantly strive to improve your skills and knowledge. The field of web development and mobile application architecture is ever-evolving, and by embracing a growth mindset, you'll be well-positioned to adapt and thrive in this dynamic landscape.

Chapter 15: Conclusion and Next Steps

As we reach the end of our journey through the process of building production-ready Flask APIs for mobile applications, it's essential to take a step back and reflect on the key concepts and techniques we've covered. In this final chapter, we'll summarize the critical aspects of ensuring robust Flask API quality, provide resources for continued learning and community involvement, and share some final thoughts on the future directions of Flask API development.

Summary of Key Concepts and Techniques

Throughout this book, we've explored a wide range of strategies and best practices for building high-quality, secure, and scalable Flask APIs to power mobile applications. Let's revisit the core concepts and techniques that have been instrumental in this endeavor:

1. **Comprehensive Testing Strategies**: We delved into the importance of implementing a comprehensive testing suite, including unit tests, integration tests, and end-to-end tests, to ensure the reliability and stability of your Flask API. By integrating these testing strategies with a Continuous Integration (CI) and Continuous Deployment (CD) pipeline, you can catch regressions early and maintain a high level of quality throughout the development lifecycle.

2. **Securing Flask APIs**: Securing your Flask API was a crucial focus, as it involves implementing robust authentication and authorization mechanisms, protecting sensitive data, and safeguarding against com-

CHAPTER 15: CONCLUSION AND NEXT STEPS

mon API vulnerabilities. We discussed best practices for token-based authentication, role-based access control (RBAC), and techniques to mitigate the impact of Denial-of-Service (DoS) attacks.

3. **Monitoring and Troubleshooting**: Effective monitoring and troubleshooting strategies are essential for maintaining the reliability and responsiveness of your Flask API. We explored the importance of comprehensive logging, error handling, performance metrics, distributed tracing, and anomaly detection, which enable you to quickly identify and resolve issues in your production environment.

4. **Extending Flask Capabilities with Extensions**: The modularity and extensibility of Flask were highlighted, as we demonstrated how you can leverage popular Flask extensions to enhance the functionality of your mobile API, covering areas like caching, task queuing, real-time updates, and RESTful API design.

5. **Versioning and Evolving Flask APIs**: Maintaining a well-defined versioning strategy and gracefully evolving your Flask API over time are crucial for ensuring a smooth integration experience for your mobile app developers. We discussed various versioning approaches, deprecation practices, and techniques to maintain backwards compatibility.

6. **Integrating Flask APIs with Mobile Frameworks**: Seamless integration between your Flask API and the mobile development frameworks used in your application (e.g., React Native, Flutter, native Android/iOS) was a key focus. We explored best practices for API design, data synchronization, and offline support to provide a cohesive and reliable experience for your mobile app users.

7. **Deploying Flask APIs to Cloud Platforms**: To ensure the scalability and reliability of your Flask API in production, we covered various deployment strategies, including containerization with Docker, managed services like AWS Elastic Beanstalk and Google App Engine, and serverless architectures using AWS Lambda and compatible frameworks.

8. **Optimization Techniques for Mobile-focused Flask APIs**: Enhancing the performance, scalability, and efficiency of your Flask API was a crucial aspect, as we discussed techniques like database optimization,

caching, asynchronous processing, and load balancing to ensure that your mobile API backend can effectively handle the demands of your application.

By mastering these key concepts and techniques, you've gained a comprehensive understanding of how to build production-ready Flask APIs that can reliably power the backend of your mobile applications, providing a seamless and responsive experience for your users.

Resources for Continued Learning and Community Involvement

As you continue your journey of building and maintaining Flask-powered mobile API backends, there are numerous resources available to help you expand your knowledge, stay updated with the latest developments, and engage with the Flask community.

1. **Official Flask Documentation**: The official Flask documentation (https://flask.palletsprojects.com/) is an invaluable resource for learning the core Flask framework, understanding its features and APIs, and exploring the best practices recommended by the Flask team.
2. **Flask Extensions Documentation**: Many of the Flask extensions covered in this book, such as Flask-SQLAlchemy, Flask-JWT-Extended, and Flask-Caching, have their own dedicated documentation that provides in-depth information on their usage and configuration.
3. **Online Tutorials and Courses**: Platforms like Udemy, Pluralsight, and Coursera offer a wide range of tutorials, courses, and video lessons on Flask development, covering various topics from beginner to advanced levels.
4. **Flask Community and Forums**: Engage with the active Flask community on platforms like Stack Overflow, GitHub, and Reddit's r/flask subreddit. These channels can be invaluable sources of information, troubleshooting help, and discussions around the latest trends and best practices in Flask development.
5. **Flask-related Books and eBooks**: There are several books and eBooks available that dive deeper into Flask development, covering specific

use cases, advanced topics, and real-world case studies. Some popular examples include "Flask Web Development" by Miguel Grinberg and "Building Modular Apps with Flask" by Daniel Gaspar.

6. **Flask Project Repositories**: Explore open-source Flask project repositories on GitHub, such as the official Flask-related projects (https://github.com/pallets) and community-driven projects, to learn from the code and design patterns used by experienced Flask developers.

7. **Flask Conferences and Meetups**: Stay connected with the Flask community by attending local and global Flask conferences, such as Flask Conference (https://www.flaskconf.com/) and Flask Europe (https://www.flaskeurope.com/). These events provide opportunities to network, learn from industry experts, and stay updated on the latest trends and best practices.

8. **Flask-related Newsletters and Blogs**: Subscribe to newsletters and follow blogs that focus on Flask development, such as The Flask Mega-Tutorial Newsletter (https://blog.miguelgrinberg.com/) and the Flask weekly newsletter (https://www.getrevue.co/profile/flask-weekly).

By leveraging these resources, you can continuously expand your knowledge, stay informed about the latest developments in the Flask ecosystem, and actively contribute to the Flask community, further enhancing your skills and expertise in building production-ready Flask APIs for mobile applications.

Final Thoughts and Future Directions for Flask API Development

As we conclude our journey through the world of building production-ready Flask APIs, it's important to reflect on the evolving landscape of web development and the role that Flask may play in the future.

Flask has firmly established itself as a popular and versatile web framework, particularly for building small to medium-sized web applications and APIs. Its simplicity, flexibility, and modular design have made it an attractive choice for developers who value a minimalist approach and the ability to customize their application stack.

In the context of mobile app development, Flask's strengths as a backend API framework are likely to continue to be relevant and valuable. As mobile apps continue to rely on robust and scalable backend services, the need for reliable and well-designed API backends will only grow. Flask's ability to be tailored to specific requirements, integrate with a wide range of extensions, and deploy to various cloud platforms make it a compelling choice for powering the backend infrastructure of mobile applications.

Moreover, the Flask community has remained active and engaged, continuously enhancing the framework, developing new extensions, and addressing evolving requirements. As new trends and technologies emerge in the web and mobile app development landscape, it will be interesting to see how Flask adapts and evolves to maintain its relevance and competitiveness.

Some potential future directions for Flask API development include:

1. **Serverless and Microservices Architectures**: As the adoption of serverless computing and microservices architectures continues to grow, Flask may see increased usage in building modular, scalable, and event-driven API backends that can seamlessly integrate with these architectural patterns.
2. **Integration with Emerging Technologies**: The Flask ecosystem may expand to include more extensions and integrations with emerging technologies, such as real-time communication frameworks, IoT platforms, and AI/ML services, allowing Flask-powered APIs to seamlessly interact with these cutting-edge systems.
3. **Performance and Scalability Enhancements**: As the demand for high-performance and highly scalable API backends continues to rise, the Flask community may focus on improving the framework's performance characteristics, exploring techniques like asynchronous programming, caching, and distributed computing to meet the needs of modern mobile applications.
4. **Security and Compliance Advancements**: With the increasing importance of data privacy and regulatory compliance in the mobile app ecosystem, the Flask community may prioritize enhancing the security features and compliance capabilities of the framework, ensuring that Flask-powered APIs can meet the stringent requirements of enterprise-

grade mobile applications.

5. **Developer Experience and Tooling Improvements**: To further streamline the development and deployment of Flask-powered APIs, the community may invest in enhancing the developer experience through improved tooling, CI/CD integrations, and seamless cloud platform integrations, making it easier for developers to build, deploy, and maintain their Flask API backends.

As you continue your journey of building and maintaining Flask-powered mobile API backends, it's essential to stay informed, adaptable, and proactive in addressing the evolving needs of your mobile applications and the wider industry trends. By embracing the strengths of Flask, leveraging the resources available, and staying engaged with the community, you'll be well-positioned to navigate the future of Flask API development and deliver high-quality, reliable, and scalable backend solutions for your mobile apps.

Conclusion

Throughout this book, we've explored the comprehensive process of building production-ready Flask APIs to power the backend of mobile applications. From mastering the fundamental Flask concepts to implementing robust testing strategies, securing your API, and optimizing its performance, we've covered a wide range of techniques and best practices to ensure the quality and reliability of your Flask-powered mobile API backends.

By applying the strategies and principles discussed in this book, you'll be equipped to build Flask APIs that can effectively and seamlessly integrate with your mobile applications, providing a seamless and responsive experience for your users. Additionally, you'll have the knowledge and tools to continuously evolve and maintain your Flask API, adapting to the changing requirements of your mobile app and the broader industry trends.

As you move forward in your journey of Flask API development, remember to stay curious, embrace learning, and actively engage with the Flask community. The field of web development and mobile application architecture is constantly evolving, and by maintaining a growth mindset, you'll be well-positioned to navigate the future and deliver innovative, reliable, and scalable backend solutions for your mobile apps.

We wish you the best of luck in your Flask API development endeavors and hope that this book has been a valuable resource in your quest to build production-ready, high-quality mobile API backends using the Flask framework.

www.ingramcontent.com/pod-product-compliance
Lightning Source LLC
Chambersburg PA
CBHW050000230526
45465CB00003BB/1185